HAIL! HAIL! UNTO THE VICTORS

Sister Thedra

Copyright © 2021 by Halls of Light, LLC

All rights reserved. This book or any portion thereof may not be reproduced or used in any manner whatsoever without the express written permission of the publisher except for the use of brief quotations in a book review.

ISBN: 978-1-7373071-0-5

To the Reader

Please read and review "Divine Explanations" on page 175 for questions and definitions of terms.

This book is only a portion of the teachings and prophecies that have been given by Sananda (Jesus Christ), Sanat Kumara, and others of the higher realms, and Recorded by Sister Thedra.

Contents

THE OPEN DOOR 1

SYMBOLS OF THE WORD 55

THEIR PROFIT 95

GATE HOUSE 147

Mission Statement 168

Sananda's Appearance 169

About the Late Sister Thedra 170

Divine Explanations 175

Other Books by TNT Publishing 186

Esu Jesus Sananda

This reproduction is from an actual photograph taken on June 1st, 1961, in Chichen Itza, Yucatan, by one of thirty archaeologists working in the area at the time. Sananda appeared in visible, tangible body and permitted His photograph to be taken.

THE OPEN DOOR

This Front piece shall be as one of the Doors - - not the two preceding ones -- This Door shall stand back of the Great Pillars - and it shall be an open door - and nothing appearing before it -- Yet in the interior shall be the words: "Hail - Hail unto the Victors" - and above that shall be the Blazing Crown of the Victor -- Let the Crown be that which stands forth - and it shall be the focal point - I shall direct thee - - fear not for I shall direct thee --

Peace - Peace - Peace -

= Time & Place =

Sori Sori -- There is but one place - one time - that is here - and now - and it is here that I say unto thee: Be ye as one blest of Me and by Me. And it is time that I give unto thee this Word:- Ye shall begin the new part by giving unto Me thy time - and the time shall be well accounted for--

Ye shall set aside the hours of five in the morning - and five in the afternoon - - and at these hours I shall bring one unto thee which shall be as thy Brother of Light - as the Elder Brother - and ye shall learn of him - and he shall place upon thy head his hand in Holy Benediction - and bless thee in Mine Name -- For I have prepared him - that he might come - and it shall profit him - and ye likewise - for it shall be profitable unto both --

Now ye shall sit with him in converse - and he shall answer thy questions - and likewise ye shall answer his -- So be it that I shall direct thee - and ye shall be as one blest - for I am with thee -- Prepare thyself for thy next part -- Ye shall now rest - and I shall touch thee - and ye shall respond unto Mine touch -- So be it and Selah --

= Porter =

Be ye as the one to receive this one which I bring at this hour - for it is for the good of all that ye receive him - for he is now prepared to give unto thee a part which shall profit them which shall accept it -- This is one which hast come unto Us from out the Galaxy - and he hast been as one afar - yet he hast the bearing of one which hast the knowledge of the Earth - and the children thereof --

The One which I now bring comes from a far and distant Star - yet ye shall come to Know him as "Neighbor" - and ye shall understand him and he shall understand thee. So be it and Selah -- For this am I bringing him unto thee - - ye shall accept him in Mine Name - for I have placed upon him Mine Seal -- So be it and Selah --

= Porter Speaks =

Be ye as one prepared to accept Me - for I come that We might have commune - and may it profit them which are prepared to receive -- So be it that I come with the consent of the Council - and it is the Great and Mighty Council - the OVER-ALL Council -- This Council of which I speak - is the One which rules over many - many - many Galaxies such as yours - and Mine - - and there is no place wherein we might go - which is not within the jurisdiction of this Council - for it is The Council of Councils --

And it behooves Me to say - that I have to pass thru this Council - for passport - that I might enter into thy place of abode -- There is a law which provides Me passport into this place wherein I am - wherein I come for this communion - and it is given unto Me to Know something of the place wherein I am - before I am allowed to enter --

Therefore I have prepared myself for entrance (much as what you would say: "a foreigner") - for I am "a foreigner" - - from afar I come - and I am come that we might know that which is to be done - and which shall be done for the time is now come when we shall work together as One - and it shall be of great profit to mankind of Earth - - and unto My people much concern -- For are not Mine people older than the Earth? and do we not see thy need - and know wherein thy strength lies?

Ye shall be as one on whose head I lay Mine hand - and I shall bless thee in Holy Benediction - and ye shall bless others as I have blest thee. So be it and Selah --

= The Calculation of Time =

For this day - let it be said that there is but little time - yet I say - we know no time - save by events - which do occur within the realms of man - and within the Cosmos -- For thy realm - the events are of shorter cycles - shorter duration - and the events of the Cosmos are of Greater duration - larger - longer cycles - and of Greater intensity -- Therefore the Great Cycles are made up of many shorter ones - which thy earthly events are but a fraction thereof --

While it is expedient that I say more on the subject of cycles - it is also necessary that I say: The events of man are small indeed - in comparison unto the Great and profound system in which "Man" hast his being -- For man is but part of the profound being which He Is - and his is but part of the Whole --

While man hast for the most part forgotten his identity and his heritage - he hast thot himself to be alone - ruler of the Earth - and the fullness thereof -- Yet he hast not Known the <u>fullness</u> thereof - for it is not yet within his knowledge that which the Earth is - - the fullness of her wealth - the strength which lies within her - the love she bears her offspring -- They give her no credit for being ensouled -- She hast brot forth as ungrateful - willful generation --

= The Green Emerald =

Yet the time cometh swiftly - when they shall see her for that which she is -- I say unto thee: We see from afar - the Earth as a small beautiful Gem - which wanders - crying from pain - and begging relief from her suffering -- So be it We come that She be relieved from such anguish.

I am but One which reaches out to assist in this - her time of trial - yet ye shall stand with Me - and <u>Know</u> ye that the Earth - shall not perish! While there shall be great upheavals - great upheavals! Great anguish - and sore trials - - She shall come thru as the Victor - for She is precious - precious in the System of Systems --

= Man in Part =

I speak of Creation - - <u>in</u> <u>the</u> <u>System</u> <u>of</u> <u>Creation</u> - within the realm of things Created by the Creator which ye call God -- which we call Solen Aum Solen -- For We see the Whole as ONE - and ye see many - many parts - and separations - while we see the wholeness of all things Created - as Whole - even as the substance from which cometh the many -- For we see the many returning unto the Substance from which it cometh - which is Light -- Light containeth the Substance from which all things are come - and unto which all "things" return -- And it is Mine part to impart unto thee - some small concept - of the part which man plays within the Whole of the Cosmos - for he is but part - and he - as "man" - is but part!

= Man's Creations =

This part which man of Earth now plays - is not his final role - for he shall again take up his role - as the part within another drama -- He shall play yet another - and another - he shall be as one well trained in each part he plays - - then he shall be as one prepared for his next role -- This is the Theater of Life - which is endless - for Life is Eternal - and the existence of Life is not denied anywhere! For that matter - Life is everywhere -- And it is said that LIFE IS - and it is given unto Me to Know - for I see as ye do not see --

    Life is Light - Light is Life - Vibrant scintillating and Alive - full of Vibrance - and it is not to be despoiled for it is the Purity of the Creative Force - the which man calls "God" -- This Creative Force is moved upon by the "Word" - and it becomes "things" tangible - and real - unto the sight and touch - and man hast claimed these as his own creation - - and in a measure he is correct - for he hast imaged himself creator of "things" -- While his imaging hast not brot him security - neither his freedom - he hast never-the-less created his many "things" - some which shall turn upon him as great monsters to devour him -- He shall come to fear his own creation - then he shall cry out for Our assistance -- Then - We shall give unto him a hand - and he shall Know that he has not "Reckoned with the Host" - for the Host moves in ways he understands not ---

= The Plan =

Man - as such - hast not come into his own - - he is as yet the child - knowing not his inheritance - - he stands as on quicksand - and he knows not his own weakness - neither his strength - for he is not yet mature - - he has not come into his own -- So be it that he shall - and he shall be as one with Great power - and then he shall Know his strength - and use it wisely - for the good of the Whole - and then he - the Man of Earth - shall be brot into the Council of which I am but One And this Council - of which I am but one small part - shall grant unto him passport beyond his present limits --

He shall be given passage unto other parts of the System of which he is part - and there shall be mutual benefits -- This is the Plan - this is the part which we are to play you and Me - - for this shall be Mine part to assist thee - to assist them This is but the beginning of Our Work for it is the first of Our Communications which shall go out unto them which are prepared to receive --

And it shall be for all which have the <u>mind</u> to receive -- Unto them which have not the mind - it shall be as a closed book - <u>un</u> <u>read</u> - and unknown - - for that matter it shall be as nothing unto them - for they haven't seen - nor heard that which is said. So let them be - and remember ye this: This is Our time - our part - and for this have we come - that it profit the "Whole"-- So be it and Selah. Let it suffice that I am One Sent - and for the sake of identification - call Me "Porter" for I stand at the Gate - and none pass without My Knowledge -- Porter

This is the hour of our communication - for <u>Our</u> communication -- So be it profitable unto each one which seeks the Light -- I say - it shall profit <u>them</u> - - let it be - so shall it be --

Now we shall continue our discourse on the part which We shall play in this - the Great Plan - which is unfolding before thee -- We shall be as far removed as the thots - from each other - - ye shall think of Me and I shall draw close unto thee - with wisdom and with Great tolerance for it is with tolerance that we come - and the Love we bear a sick and troubled people --

This is the way we see the mankind of Earth -- They cry out for help! Wherein have they found it? Wherein have they heeded the Voice of Assistance? Wherein have they given heed unto the Voice of Silence? The Voice of their own conscience hast spoken within them - and they have not heeded that! for they have gone headlong into the pit --

Now that they cry out - we have come that we might assist -- While it is unlawful for us to do that which is given unto them to do - we shall teach them how to do that which they shall do for themself --

= To Each His Own =

We carry not their "pots"-- We are part of the Whole - yet the hand does not the work of the foot - neither the hand the work of the eye -- Neither do we the work which is Mans' - for he hast the idea - the time and the energy given unto him - that he learn to use such tools wisely --

The Earth being a School room - a laboratory - wherein he might work out his problems - he hast but to turn unto the Light - and benefit by the problems afront -- And he shall be the better for the solution thereof - "A lesson learned - is truly a lesson earned"--

It is said: "Ye shall prove thy worth" and it is so - for it is the law - that as one is prepared - so shall he become --

This is the Great lesson man needs learn - for he hast been remiss - in that he hast not prepared himself for the Greater things - that he live in peace with his brothers - that he be as one prepared for the day which is now upon him --

= Pollution =

He has "fiddled" and danced to his own merry tune - while his world is suffocating! Suffocating! I say - Suffocating! - for he knows not that he hast polluted both the air and the Earth beneath his feet - as well as the minds of men -- The children yet unborn shall die in infancy for their wonton - for their carelessness - and they shall be as ones on whose shoulders rest Great responsibility - and they shall learn well the lesson of: That which goes out shall return - even as it went out -- That which is created perfect shall return perfect - for no contamination shall enter into the place wherein they <u>HOPE</u> - to enter - - for therein is no impurities - no contamination --

= Thought =

Now let us consider:-

That which is Eternal is Eternal - and that which is matter is but conditioned by thot – thot made manifest -- And the thot which holds that which is made manifest - shall be withdrawn - and it - the thing manifest - shall no longer be seen of man- for it shall be as nothing - and no more shall it be - for the thot which hast held it in form shall simply be withdrawn - and it - the manifestation shall be no more --

So be it that all thots first have their origin in the Light - for thot is Light - Light Substance - and no man hast truly measured Light Substance - for the Substance of Light can neither be measured -

weighed - nor calculated by man -- Light is the unknown quantity - the unknown factor - which brings forth the manifestation of all things - be it human form - or a tree - - even the stone -- And it is given unto Me to Know that which is Created - yet I do not presume to know what Light Substance is - - for that matter - I do not know what Life is - for that and Light are of the Same Essence --

= The Riddle of Life =

Beyond that we do not Know - the reason - that which causes Life to be -- Yet some call it Life - and are done with it - yet the riddle is not solved - - it is not solved by being content with such names as "Life" - "God" - the mysterious names -- To Know Life - and to Know God - is the direction every man sets for himself - to return unto his origin -

= The Mariner =

What mattereth the Name? It is the direction which he sets for himself. Whither he goeth he knows not - he walks blindly - yet he sets his sails homeward - obeying the laws set before him -- For it is the way of the Mariner to set his compass by the Star - and it is the Star which guides him - - the compass but his instrument - by which he is directed to the course -- And he hast lost sight of his guiding Star - therefore his compass is of no use - for he sees not the Star - upon which to set his course --

There are blind mariners - which know in which direction they go for they see with the eye of Spirit - <u>The eye of Spirit</u> - and they are in no need of the instrument - the thot manifestation - - they have thot with the Greater <u>Mind</u> - greater power - greater wisdom of things Eternal - and they have placed before them the things Eternal - which shall not perish - or pass away -- These have set their sails into the Sunrise of a New day - and they shall not fail their course - - for they shall return unto their abiding place - unharmed - unscathed -- So be it I shall continue this discourse in the early hours of morning -- So be ye as one blest to receive Me --

= I am "Porter" =

(I come to this trysting place - while Teresa is in labor in another room.)

Sori Sori -- I come unto thee this minute - that ye be as one prepared for thy next part - for it shall be as none other -- The part which shall be given unto thee is the part which is new and different -- There shall be the ones which come unto thee crying for help - and they shall be as ones prepared to receive it - for they shall be as ones in need - and for <u>that</u> ye shall give unto them assistance - and they shall be as ones blest This is Mine word unto thee at this minute - So be it and Selah – wait.

Be ye as Mine hand made manifest - and give unto them this Word and it shall go into the record - and it shall stand for all time -- That which is said unto thee here is for the record - and it shall be for the generation which is now come -- Yet the next generation shall bear witness of Mine Words - and that which is recorded herein -- They shall be blest by the presence of the one which hast come into embodiment thru the womb of flesh this day --

They shall be as ones prepared to receive this one - and she shall be called blessed - for hers is a part separate from any other -- Yet it is said her name shall not be considered greatest among women - - however - she shall be as one which hast Mine hand upon her - for she shall be blest of Me - and by Me - for it is thru and by the Council that she comes into flesh - - born of woman tho she be -- She shall be as one which walks Knowingly - and she shall be as one on whose head I place Mine hand in Holy Benediction - and I shall be unto her all the Father would have Me be. So be it I shall speak of this one again -- So be it and Selah --

= The Infant =

God-father

Sori Sori -- This would I say unto thee at this hour: This is one which has come unto thee for a mighty work - and it is given unto Me to Know - for I have been as One with her - she hast been with Me - and it shall be as Mine hand is upon her --

I shall lead - and guide her into paths of righteousness - yet - she shall be as one of flesh - and she shall not be favored - for she shall be <u>as</u> <u>one</u> of flesh and bone - and come under the law of flesh - - for this hast she taken upon herself flesh. She shall be blest of Me and by Me - for I shall stand watch - I shall sponsor her - and be unto her as the Father would have Me be -- Let us say - I shall play - "god-father" unto her - and none shall take that part from Me - for have I not known her for long? I see her as she is - and for what she is - - not for the infant that she appears to be -- Be ye aware of that which she is - so be it ye shall be blest -- So be it and Selah --

= Cycles - Cause & Effect =

Sori Sori -- It is Mine time to speak of things to come - and it shall be as nothing before - for it is given unto Me to see the records of events and it is said: We tell time by the Great events - and no event takes place without its cause -- When the effect is seen -or come about - we see it as done - or finished - a new cycle beginning -- And it is now come when one cycle endeth and another beginneth -- This one just ended - is but the intermediate - with which ye of Earth are concerned for thy time extendeth yet into the beginning of the new and larger cycle of time --

This is the time which hast been foretold - when they shall stand in want - and cry for assistance - when there shall be great suffering and sorrow --

Yet this is the fulfilling of the old cycle which is now ending and which overlaps the new - even as a chain linked one link with the other - and each link belonging unto the other by virtue of <u>being</u> a chain for the chain is made up of links - each cycle made up of events - one linked unto the other - and each the fulfilling of a law of cause and effect - - each being the manifestation of thot - - such is the Idea - for the Idea first is thot - - the manifestation follows the thot --

= The Immaculate Concept =

Now let it be as the law provides - for it is given unto Me to see the "Idea" as perfect -- Thot manifests in matter - and becomes real unto thee - which are children of Earth -- Now it is Mine part to give unto thee a part which shall first begin with the IDEA - - then thru thot it becomes made flesh - - made manifest - seen - of men --

So be it that there are few who Know the "IDEA" behind the manifestation -- So be it I shall speak of this thot process at our next meeting -- So be it I shall take leave of thee at this hour -- So be it and Selah --

= The Word Immaculate =

Sori Sori -- This is the Word I would give unto thee this day: There is but the thot made manifest in the world of men - and it is from the parent idea - and the parent of the Idea is the Word Immaculate - - it is the forerunner of All materialization -- The Idea is first created by the Immaculate Word Sent forth thru thot - thot becomes - that which is made manifest unto the physical eye and touch --

It is vibration from the first - slowed down unto sight - and in its vibrancy - which is in the unseen - it is not possible for the eye of man to see - - yet as it is slowed down - mans' eyes become sensitized unto it -- This is a crude way of saying that which is impossible to convey in words -- So be it that we shall improve as we proceed with these discourses -- Thereby - let us give an example:

When the wheel is first spinning - it is clearly seen -- When it gains its maximum speed - it is unseen by thy eyes - yet it is the reverse with the Idea - conceived in the mind of the Infinite - for the Idea was there always - and it was known and seen in the place wherein all things are known -- <u>Then</u> it is slowed down as it goes forth into time and space - <u>fainter/</u> slower it becomes as it goes within the mind of men –

Therefore it becomes contaminated by mans' mind/ thinking/ opinions for he hast not the mind to receive the Thot - or Idea in its purity - or in the Immaculate state - uncontaminated by error - - for man fumbles and errors in his search for truth - for he hast recorded within his mind so many errors - since he first went out from his original place of abode.

So be it that I shall speak of this again - when ye have had more rest. So be it we shall wait -

Recorded by Sister Thedra

The following is in answer to my question - how to answer one who has asked (in part):

"What is the fastest way for me to prepare my earthly vehicle? Is there a special Sibor whose part it is to help those of us who are here from other planets - to tune our bodies? Is there a special one who will help me to quicken this flesh so that my whole consciousness can begin work on this plane?"

* * *

There are none which take the Gates of Heaven by force -- They which are anxious shall find that they wait - even as the sleepers - for they have as yet not learned that which I have given unto them --

They shall be as ones prepared -- There are no short ways - no easy way It is the way of the dragon to promise the ease - and pleasure -- Be not concerned with their haste - - give unto them that which I have prepared for them - and let them find their way - - so be it they shall profit thereby Give unto them that which I have given unto thee for them - - KEEP for thyself that which I have given unto thee - - for it is for thine own sake that I have given unto thee that which is for thee alone - none other, for they would but rend thee --

Such is Mine Word unto thee --

Sori Sori -- Mine Beloved:- It is the call which is heard and answered that matters - for I have put within thy hand certain things to do - and thou hast done them - and thou hast not wearied of Mine Work -- Now ye shall be at peace and fear not - for I see thee and know thee for that which ye are - - and no place have ye failed in that which ye have been given to do -- So be it ye shall now be prepared to receive the One which comes from Afar – and he shall be as one tolerant for thy tardiness – Ye shall be as one which has held thine own counsel – and ye have done that which wast given unto thee to do – So be ye as one blest of Me and by Me--

= Systems of Communications =

Sori Sori -- Be ye as one prepared to receive Me - and ye shall be blest of Me -- So be it and Selah -- There shall be others which shall come - even as I - and they shall add their part unto Mine - and ye shall be as one prepared to commune with them - - it shall profit both - and ye shall come to know them - and they shall know thee as they have not known thee --

This I would say unto thee: The method in which we communicate is but by thot -- We have an idea - it is thot thru according unto fulfillment - and the thot becomes transferred in the etheric waves - and enters into thy mind as word symbols -- It is within thy own mind that these symbols are transposed from the original idea - therefore it is necessary that we use the symbols which correspond unto thy own native tongue - and which is rapidly transferable or translated - This is one system -- Another system which we use is the sight -- It is by being shown certain symbols - which you can easily translate -- While not always easily - or correctly translated - they bring with them certain revelation or understanding --

Therefore we shall use both systems - which shall hasten very efficiently - the work which we shall do -- This is by no means the least of the work - - while it is not the greatest - - the Greater part is yet before us -- This is but the beginning of this Our part together - for there are others which shall be brot into the plan as it now exists - - as they are now being prepared for the parts which shall be given unto them -- And as they are prepared - so shall it be revealed unto them - that which they shall do -- So be it and Selah --

This is the first of the activity of this kind which is now being brot forth -- As the Plan unfolds - more shall be brot into the service which we shall render unto the sick - sad world -

For - it shall be given the part of protection - and it shall be blest in its part - for it - the world - the <u>Earth</u> shall be healed of her infirmity and malfunctions-- She - the Earth - shall rejoice for her healing - and she shall be as the woman delivered of child - for She shall be cleansed and purified -- So be it and Selah --

Ye shall rest thy body - and fret not for the small things - and all shall be well -- So be it I am come that it be so -- Be ye at peace -

= Honor Thy Father & Mother =

Sori Sori -- "Honor thine Father and Mother" hast been a cliché' - with many in the world of men - yet it is said - they shall come into the place of their going out - perfect - even as they went out - for none shall return unprepared --

= Do with Wisdom =

They shall return unto Him in Honor and in Glory -- So be it, it is given unto Me to say unto thee: Do that which is given unto thee to do - with dignity and purpose - that purpose being - to honor and serve Him the Father - the Source of thy being -- Let it ever be thy purpose to serve Him - by lifting up all beings - - and none shall be as the lesser - none the greater -- Yet it is said: Ye shall Know that which ye are to do - - ye shall "DO" with <u>wisdom</u> - and Know what thou art about -- Ye shall not contribute unto their slothfulness - their delinquency - their ignorance of the law --

= Example =

Ye shall be unto them a living example of a Son of God -- Ye shall walk upright with head high - knowing thyself to be a "Son of God" - for I say it is an honor to be <u>Made</u> a "Son of God" - and that by adoption. While there are Sons of God by Birth Right - these have gone out from Him pure and perfect - and have never taken upon themself the body of flesh - neither have they been defiled or contaminated by the world of flesh -- And this shall be as the first contamination - when they take upon themself the animal flesh body --

This is their first fall - and it is given unto Me to know whereof I speak -- This is the first fall - for the flesh is the contaminated form - in which the pure in heart enter - which then comes to know itself as Man of flesh -- And this "man of flesh" loses his identity as he enters into the earth vibration - - into the earth vibrations he comes as one pure -- While he forgets his identity for a time - he is constantly reminded of his Source - by the way of contact with his Source - and his Guide - his Mentor - his constant Companion Yet - it is said - they forget in <u>time</u>

that they are in contact with their Source - and they seek direction of men of flesh - thereby losing their way -- So be it that they shall again seek their Source - and then they shall find that they are One with IT - with Him the Father --

So be it - that One shall be near - to remind him that he is One in Him, his Source and that he hast but to remember his being One in Him, of Him - and then he shall turn unto Him - and be glad that he Knows from whence he came - and whither he goest -- So be it that I am come that there be greater understanding amongst men - of the world - for it is expedient that they know that they are not alone - cast out - without Father or Mother - that they are not outcasts - without home - or Brothers who care --

= One Which Cares =

I say: I am One which cares - and I am come that they Know - that they might be prepared for Greater things -- So be it that I am come from a far and distant land - even beyond thy own Galaxy - and for this have I come - that ye of Earth might break away thy legirons - and soar unto unknown heights with Me - and be as the Light unto the firmaments which bear witness of Greater things than Man - than the world of men.

While it is no little part that ye of Earth now play - I say: It is but the first of a Greater play - which ye are now part of -- The preparation here - now - is but the rehearsal of the next part - and I say unto thee: Be ye aware of thine part - know well thy lines - forget not thy part -- Be ye as one responsible for that which ye do - and be as one prepared to receive the reward for thy past services rendered -- Be ye alert - and responsive unto the WORD - given unto thee for the purpose of enlightening thee - - that is the purpose for which it is given -- Lift up thy feet - and move forth in thanksgiving - and do honor unto them which give of themself that ye be lifted up --

Bless thyself to move out of thy tracks - and be ye as one responsible for the way in which ye go - for it is given unto thee to choose thy own way -- This is given unto thee - for thou hast been given the Gift of free will - and none shall take from thee thy choice -- Now bear in mind that I come as One prepared to serve thee in wisdom and love - yet I bear not thy form - neither shall I take upon Myself the form of man -- I have form - I am form - yet I am more than form - for I am the form - and the form is Me --

Yet I say - I am not the form - I am the Spirit - and the form is animated by that which I Am -- And it is given unto Me to be as One enabled to take upon Mineself any form I might choose - that I might give unto thee a certain lesson - in wisdom - - never - to satisfy thy curiosity - or to demonstrate Mine power - <u>Or</u> to give unto thee proof of Mine power - for that is not Mine purpose --

Mine purpose is to enlighten and assist them with a purpose - and that is to honor the Father and Mother from which they come -- So be it I shall find them - and I shall single them out - and give unto them as they are able to receive -- So be it and Selah -- So let it be for the Good of All --

I Am

= In Mine Father's House are Many Mansions =

Sori Sori -- This is Our time for communion - and it is for this that I come - and it is given unto Me to be the One called Porter - for I am the Porter at the Gate - and it is by Me that ye pass from thy own Galaxy unto the next - for I am set over the entrance thru which ye pass from thine own into Mine -- And it shall be given unto thee to Know Me as ye come into the place wherein I abide - and thru which ye shall pass - While it is said - ye shall pass thru the passage way - it is by Me that ye pass - for I am set over the entrance into the place wherein they go - which are free to enter --

These which are free to enter - shall find Me at the Entrance -- Even as the One - Sananda - stands Porter at the Gate for thy own Galaxy - So - do I stand porter at Mine -- Ye shall be as one free to pass - for it is said - thy passport is in order -- So be it and Selah --

I am the One which shall stand sponsor for thee - and ye shall Know Me as I am - and ye shall be glad - - so be it I shall be glad --

Wherein is it said that each and every one shall be prepared for his part -- We are now making known unto thee thy part - for it is no small part which ye have been given -- For it is as planned - and prophesied of old - - for that matter it is now come when they shall behold the Hand of God move - and they shall read that which is Eternally Written - and no hand shall obliterate it from the pages of time - for time shall reveal all that is written as Truth - and Truth cannot be obliterated or changed for IT IS - and shall ever remain TRUTH --

So be it I speak not in riddles - neither in parables - yet thou knowest not that which I say - for it is yet before thee - as much as the morrow - for thou hast not seen the fulfillment of Mine Word - neither understandeth thou Mine saying. So be it that I am come that ye might have understanding -- So be it and Selah --

= Our Part in the Divine Plan =

For this day let us consider the part given us - and that which shall be accomplished --

The way in which it shall be accomplished shall be natural unto us and as it is natural unto us - and unto our understanding - yet we do not always understand that which is being accomplished in the doing -- For our parts shall be put with other parts - that they fit into the Whole Plan Therefore we shall put them all together - before we see the fulfillment of the Plan --

This is the part which you and Me have - is to bring together your part and Mine - that others be fit in - and then the Greater understanding of that which is now being done - or accomplished --

The way of man is the way of flesh - and flesh is restless and inquisitive - and it is curious about the outcome - and fretful for each part -- While it is given unto us to be patient - and fret not for the outcome - for we see it as finished -- While we wait with patience the outcome - we are prepared for that which we shall do - and we are mindful of man's impatience - his blunders and weakness -- It is the way of flesh to blunder - therefore we have great compassion - and tolerance for him in his effort - for we see him fall - pick himself up and try again -- So be it we are the older - and the wiser - having been the ones which have gone before thee in aeons ago -- We are now as thine Elders - prepared to assist thee in thine Graduation from thine own "School of Earth" -- This is the way of the Elders -- to lead - guide and Direct the Younger Bretheren - yet in swaddling clothes - for the most part --

This is the Word I would give unto thee: There is the part which is given unto each and every one which comes into flesh - and he shall do that <u>part</u> with the purpose for which it is given unto <u>it</u> --The parts shall fit as One Whole - and it shall be the fulfilling of a Plan - designed to lift man above the animal - above his present existence - his present understanding of himself or his present abode -- For he shall come into Greater understanding of his being/ of himself / of his part - and therefore he shall find that he is put into his proper place - wherein he fits --

When it is come that he leaves the flesh - he shall find he hast a place prepared - wherein he shall fit - and be at home - even tho he knows not that he is not yet in flesh - even tho he knows not that he is no more of the flesh - he shall be as he was - in Spirit - and Spirit shall be conscious of itself as being -- Yet it is said: "Spirit sleepeth" - it is so - therefore Spirit sleepeth in flesh - and it is Mine part to awaken Spirit -- "Spirit of Man Come Forth! as Spirit - and be ye as the Light which dwelleth Eternally in the Heavens" - Such is the Call I send forth this day: "Come ye forth as Awake! Speak - O Spirit!"-- Let the flesh be flesh -- Let Spirit be Spirit - and let the Spirit rejoice that it hast heard -- Let flesh obey that which Spirit hast spoken - that Spirit hast heard -- So be it that the awakening hast begun - and man hast begun to stir - - for this I am glad -- So be it I shall speak unto thee again at the hour designated - and ye shall rest and prepare thyself for thy part. So be it and Selah --

While it is yet early in the day - ye shall put thyself within thy place wherein ye shall rest and be at peace --So be it I shall be unto thee Great assistance ---

= Raphael Speaks of the "Tiny" =

Sori Sori -- Mine hour hast come when I shall speak for Mine own - for I come as the Voice of many - which stand watch with Me -- And We would say with one Voice - that ye have done well - - ye have received unto thyself one which hast come - and one which is sent - - even as an infant hast she come - and it is given unto us to see the way in which she hast been received - in which she is received -- So be it that this little one is <u>not</u> the little one - for we know her not as the little one - for she is the one which hast come unto thee - into thy midst - as one full of Grace - and she shall bless them with whom she shall abide -- She shall be given a part which none other shall have - and none shall take from her the part which she hast chosen --

This little tiny - as ye see her - is but the flesh - for ye see not the Spirit behind the manifestation of flesh - the so-called Miracle -- While it is not seen by thee - that which is back of the manifestation - I say: Great Ones attended the birth of this tiny one - and she too - attended her own birth -- Think ye not that Spirit is bound in the tiny - in flesh form - for the Beloved One stands ever watchful - that this tiny one be as one protected and wanted - for it is given unto some to be unwanted,- uncared for - and for this do they suffer --

This is another Story - to be told later -- While We shall continue with this one which we now speak of as the "tiny one"-- She shall not remain nameless - yet it is said her name shall not be the greatest known unto man -- yet she shall be honored amongst women - for she shall do a work yet unknown unto woman -- And her name shall be known within the Book of Life - for it is written there - and she shall do that which she hast come to do - and she shall fulfill her part of the Plan -- So be it she shall walk with the famous - and near famous - and she shall be as one on whose shoulders shall fall great responsibility - for she shall be as one prepared for such responsibility -- and it shall be unto the Glory of the One which stands Sponsor for her -- And it is Mine place to say: She shall walk as one in flesh - she shall come under the law of flesh- she shall do that which is given unto the one of flesh - and she shall be no exception --

She shall be in no wise different from any other - for she shall do that which is given unto ones of flesh -- Yet I say - she shall **be** different from all others - in-as-much as she has a part to play - and play it she shall - for this is she come at this time -- So be it - I have spoken and thou hast heard Me -- So be it recorded for the record - and it shall go into the present book now being prepared -- So be it that it shall profit them which receive this part - to take it unto themself - and read with eyes of Spirit - and See with the eye of Spirit, what Spirit hath said -- So be it I am Raphael –

= Mother & Child =

Such would I say unto the children of Earth at this time: The Earth is now going thru the birth pangs - which shall be unto her much agony - and for this hast there come from afar - One which shall assist her - for she shall be delivered - and she shall be purged and cleansed - purified healed - for she too shall be torn - and worn - as one weary -- She shall rest - and be refreshed - and then she shall rejoice in the Child which She hast borne -- For the "Child" shall bring honor unto the parent which hast born it -- It - the Child - shall Know its Mother - and glorify her -- This I would have ye know now - that the way of the Mother - is to love and adore her child - - but the child which hast been within the bosom of the Earth for long - hast not honored the mother - neither the father which hast spawned it - for it is the wayward child - - drunken on new wine it is - drunken on new wine I say! and it reels too and fro knowing not its direction - knowing not its heritage --

Now I say: It is a bastard son that the Earth hast brot forth - which shall be cast out - dis-inherited - in disgrace - no more to walk with Sons of God - no more to torment the children of men - for he - the "Bastard Son" shall be sent forth as one in disgrace - for he hast led the Sons of men astray and deceived them -- So be it that they shall come to know him for the deceiver which he is - and he shall be as one cast into utter darkness - for darkness shall be his lot - and no more shall he walk the Earth - to mock the children of men - for he hast had his day - and he hast had his way with the sons of men - and no place hast he given unto them comfort - or protection from the darkness -- He hast trapt them - he hast led them down into destruction - he hast led them into the pit -- Now I see them standing with feet on the edge of the pit while the Voice cries out: "Halt! Halt! Halt! for destruction lieth before thee!!"--

They have been as ones caught up short - and they have heard -- Now we shall give unto these assistance - ere they drop headlong into the pit --

The pit? ye ask - - the pit is that which is the pit - wherein there is no light - wherein there is no hope - wherein is no turning point! the point of no return --

This is the way of the deceiver - to lead unto destruction - wherein they find no hope -- So be it that I say: It shall end! End it shall - and for this do I now speak out - that there be understanding - and that the way be prepared before thee -- So be it that I am One of many which cries out on behalf of the Earth and her progeny -- I am now forerunner of others yet to come - and ye shall receive them unto thyself as Bretheren from afar - and such they are -- So be it and Selah --

= The Time & Idea =

Sori Sori -- This is My time - for I shall speak with thee of the time and the idea -- For the time is come when the Idea shall be sent forth as thot and it shall be as a great stimulant unto man -- There shall be great rumors of peace - and no peace shall they have -- While it is said - they search within the books for peace - the way in which to find peace - - it is given unto us to see them reject - for the most part - the IDEA OF PEACE - and they give unto others credit for the war - and restlessness they give unto the others credit for <u>No</u> peace - - they are wont to give unto themself credit for <u>No</u> peace --

For they have not found Peace within <u>their hearts</u> - where peace shall first be established - <u>THEN</u> it shall be established within and about them - their environment - and they shall radiate peace - for <u>they first</u> shall <u>be</u> at peace--

This is the way of Peace - and they shall come to know that it is not so many words on paper -- Their treaties have been broken - and are broken - and are worthless! When it becomes part of them - written within the heart - <u>THEN</u> they shall find Peace part of them - part of themself - which shall not be necessary to put on paper - neither shall it be broken -- And at no time shall it be necessary to say: We "Believe in Peace" - for it shall be expressed in action - and deed - as well as words --

The time is now come when they shall comply with the law -- They shall be as "ONE" - or they shall be separated - and no more shall they come together - for the ones which are of Peace - shall be far removed and they shall find Peace - and the warriors shall be removed into a place wherein they shall torrent themselves until they weary of it -- <u>Then</u> - they shall turn from their way and seek the Light - <u>Then</u> they shall find It - and be as ones assisted -- So be it - and Selah --

By the hand of Me shall they find the Light - shall they be assisted and it is So - for I have spoken the Word - So shall it Be --

= The Walls Shall Come Tumbling Down =

Sori Sori -- This is our time - time for this our communication - wherein we shall be as of one mind - one thot - one purpose -- This I would say unto thee: There is but few which are prepared to be one with Me in purpose - one in mind - for they are wont to look to and fro - for that which would appeal unto the eye - that which would satisfy their curiosity - and give solace unto their weary mind --

Wherein is it said - that we come to satisfy their curiosity - or give comfort unto their wants? It is said: We come that they be brot out of bondage - out of their ignorance - which is indeed bondage!

Therefore we come as with one purpose - we deviate not from the purpose - we come that they be meted out - as the law provides - as it is expedient - as they are prepared to receive --

This is the day in which the Veil shall be rent - and they shall see beyond - that which hast been hidden up -- And they shall be as ones prepared to step thru - and return into the world of men - that they report that which they have learned - for I say unto thee: The "Walls shall come tumbling down" and no longer shall they be a barrier between thee and Me - for ye shall come to Know Me even as I Know thee - and ye shall be glad -- So be it and Selah --

= Who Made the Wall? =

This I would have them know - that there is no wall - except man's own wall - which he hast builded - block by block -- He hast prepared his own wall - now he is confronted with it - and it is said - he shall climb over it - even as he hast builded it - block by block -- For he hast built it for a period of time - - now again he shall find that time is an element in his world - which he has to reckon with --

He shall in time remove - or surmount each block - block by block - then he shall see and know that he - he alone - hast built his own wall - that "impenetrable" wall which he hast seen as impassable -- Impassable? not so! I say: He shall penetrate the "impassable" barrier - and then - he shall see that it is as nothing - for he shall be as one free of his illusions - for he hast builded of illusions - and his illusions have bound him -- I now say unto thee: Be ye as one free - pass ye the barrier - and see that which hast been hidden from man --

Yet it is for this that I come - that all men might come and see - and Know -- So be it that they are not as yet prepared for such revelation - - I say: "Come ye up higher stand with Me on the Summit and See!"- I am He - which is Sent that ye be free of all boundaries - all fetters-- Come and journey with Me into realms yonder and Know ye freedom - such as I Know - - be ye as one blest to Know. So be it and Selah --

= Communication =

Mine time is come that I speak unto thee of the way in which we communicate - one with the other -- The thot is sent forth - - as thot does not travel - as such - it is pulsation however - and it is picked up - so to speak - by the one which is prepared to receive it -- It - the thot - is first conceived in the mind of the one which is the sender - or the parent of the thot - and it becomes the Word which ye record - - it becomes the Word - and is recorded - then it is put into the eth as sound when it is spoken - by you the receiver -- For this is it necessary that it be read aloud - for the benefit of the unseen ones which come to learn of us - that which shall profit them -- as they gather round about for their lessons - which they too shall learn from these communications - These communications are for the unseen ones - as well as for the ones which ye see -- This is Mine Word unto thee at this hour --

Bless thyself this day - and rest thy body - and I shall speak at another hour this day -- So be it profitable unto each one - and unto All.

Recorded by Sister Thedra

= The Action =

Sori Sori -- The time comes swiftly when we shall stand as One upon the High Holy Mt - and see from afar that which hast been done in the hours of the darkness - which hast surrounded the work of the Initiate The Work hast gone on in the hours between evening and the dawn -- It is said - the dawn cometh with great speed - and it is so - - so let us go forth as One - and no more shall we stumble in the darkness -- So be it that it is given unto Me to see them stumble - in fear - and in want.- There is nought to fear - nought to say - that hast not been said --

It is now time to act - and act we shall - for it is for this that we say: "Prepare thyself" - - it is the part of preparation - "The Action"--

We say: The time of action is come - and it shall be as nothing before - for the Action shall be of a positive nature - and it shall prove fruitful -- So let it be for the Good of All - - So shall it be --

= Come - See – Know =

Come See - Come See - and be enlightened -

Come See - Know - and be enlightened -

Come - See and be ye enlightened --

This I would say unto thee: Come - See - and Know -- This I would have thee Know: There is much to Know - much to learn - much to do. And not one place there be - wherein ye shall go which is not as a school for thy enlightenment - for thy progress --

Now I stand as One prepared to give unto thee that which is expedient for thy progress -- And no pen can record that which is to be done - neither can words convey that which lies before thee -- Ye shall be as one prepared aforehand - and ye shall step forth as one prepared to enter into thine next part - and it shall be the Greater part -- Harken unto Me - Harken unto Mine Word - and be ye as one prepared - for I say: Ye shall come into the place wherein I am - as one prepared - and then ye shall return unto them - and give unto them as ye have received. So be it and Selah - - Papa

= New Way of Life =

Sori Sori -- This is Mine hour - Mine time with thee -- This time hast thou set aside for Me - therefore I come at the appointed time - that we might have this communion - and for this I am glad -- By Mine hand I shall lead thee afar - and ye shall see and hear and Know -- Ye shall know which ye see - and ye shall return to tell of thy experiences -- Now ye shall prepare thyself for a part new and strange unto thee - and ye shall be as one strong - and as one prepared for that which shall be given unto thee to do -- No man hast seen - neither heard - nor recorded that which ye shall see and record -- So be it that we shall do a new thing - unknown unto another which shall read - for it shall be the beginning of a New time - a New day - a New way of life - for none as yet have done that which shall be given unto thee to do - and it shall be for the Good of All Mankind -- So be it and Selah --

I am come that this be the way - that this be done - that the way be made clear -- And it is given unto thee to be as one prepared to go with Me - wherein I shall lead thee -- So be it I say: Come - and Know! So be it ye shall be as one fearless - dauntless - and ye shall be as one prepared - - let it profit thee -- so be it - - Amen and Selah --

* * *

Sori Sori -- Ye shall come to Know Who is Who - and What is What - and ye shall have no need for the pen - neither for purse -- For it is now come when we shall come unto thee - as ones known unto thee - and ye shall not want or need - for it shall be given unto thee to be supplied for all thy needs shall be met -- So be it and Selah --

* * *

Sori Sori -- This is the time ye have waited for - and it is now come when ye shall be as one brot into the place wherein I am - and ye shall See and Know that which ye See --- So be it and Selah -- Ye shall have that which is kept for thee - and ye shall be blest -- So be it and Selah.

* * *

Sori Sori -- Be ye as one prepared - for this shall be the part for which ye have waited -- Ye shall partake of the Cup which I proffer unto thee. So be it and Selah -- wait -

* * *

= Portencia =

Sori Sori --This is the word I would give unto thee - - it is for this that I come -- The One which is called "Porter is for this moment standing aside - that I might speak - and it is Mine part to say: Be ye blest of Me for this do I come - that ye be blest - for I am One which He hast spoken of - that you might be prepared to receive Me -- This shall be the beginning of our communications -- That which now seems strange unto you - shall become familiar to you - and it shall become real and natural --

So be it I shall await another time - and I shall prepare a part for you - and it shall be as Mine and none other -- While this comes thru another - that which I shall prepare - shall come direct - even as that which comes of "Porter"- that is best - the direct communication - which I shall establish for the days ahead - ye might call Me porter -- While I am not the One which hast spoken as "Porter" - I come that ye might enter into the place wherein I abide -- So let it be said - I am

Portencia -- This shall be symbolmatic of our communications - - some not to be shared - some may be given unto the ones prepared - -

* * *

Sori Sori -- Be ye as one prepared for that which shall be done - and ye shall receive that which shall be given unto thee -- So be it that there shall be the ones which shall stand by to assist - and they shall be as ones prepared - for they shall know their parts well - and for this are they sent to assist -- Know ye this: That they shall be as Brothers - and they shall not fail thee -- So be it and Selah -- Let this be understood - that there are many which are with thee - that = ye be prepared -- So be it that the Way of the Lord is made open before thee - and ye shall enter into the Way thereof -- It is said: Ye shall enter into the Holy of Holies and ye shall be as one blest -- This is the Word I would leave with thee this day -- So be it and Selah --

Sanat Kumara

Sori Sori -- Beloved: It is for Me to say - that it is now come when ye shall be led out into far fields - wherein ye shall view the part which hast been accomplished - and see and know that which is to be accomplished -- And for that shall ye better do that which is to be done Ye shall be as one blest to Know - and ye shall learn that which ye shall .do aforehand -- Ye shall no longer walk blindly - knowing not - for ye shall see and Know -- So be it and Selah --

* * *

Sori Sori -- Hear ye this - and fear not - for I say unto S thee: Ye shall be as one blest to wait for that which I have for thee -- So be it that I am with thee - and ye shall be blest of Me and by Me -- So be it and Selah --

* * *

Sori Sori -- This I would say unto thee at this time: There are many which stand by that they be prepared to speak - - yet they are not permitted at this time - for it is not yet time -- The time shall come when ye shall receive them - and know each as he shall know thee -- So be it that they wait -- And it is for this that ye too shall wait - for it is now come that ye wait - for there is yet other work to be done-- So be it and Selah --

= Midnite =

Sori Sori -- For this hour let it be said - that I am with thee - and ye shall be as one prepared for that which shall be given unto thee to do - and ye shall do it with Grace and dignity - and ye shall be glad for thy preparation -- So be it and Selah -- Walk ye with dignity - and be ye as one on whose head I place Mine hand - and be ye blest - for I shall bless thee -- See ye the hand of God move - - Know ye that it moves and be ye as one blest to See -- So be it and Selah --

= Give with Wisdom =

Sori Sori -- Be ye as the hand of Me made manifest - and record this Mine Word - and it shall profit them to receive it in Mine Name -- So be it and Selah --

This I would say unto them which are fortuned to receive the Word which is designed for them -- Be there ones which are now close unto thee - for the purpose of enlightening thee - - they are sent that there be greater Light - greater understanding - and greater strength - - for that are they gathered unto the place wherein they are - that they might go forth in full armor - in strength - and wisdom - KNOWING well their part - that each one which seeks the Light might be enlightened - and prepared for greater things/ greater work/ greater Revelations -- And for this do We the Host stand ready to give of Ourself that each one be served - according to his capacity to receive --

This is the way in which the "AWAKENING" shall take place -- It is said - it shall be natural and without shock - yet - not without surprise and with Great Wisdom shall it be carried out - for without the assistance of the Host - it would not be possible -- The Host is the means thru which they which sleep shall be awakened - for the Host is made up of many - many - which have come unto us from the realm of flesh of the Earth - and they know from whence they come -- They Know the way of flesh - and the way of Earth man -- They understand him - his ways - his trials/ his errors/ his hopes/ his wants and needs --

They seek to assist them which are in need - and the ones which cry out for assistance -- These shall receive their assistance according to their capacity to receive - they shall be blest to receive - and they shall be as ones which shall be blest to Know from whence cometh their help.

Now it behooves thee to give as ye have received - with Wisdom. Let not the slothful rob thee of thy inheritance - let not the slothful drag thee down to defeat --

Give with Wisdom I say! and ye shall say unto them as I have said unto thee: "Prepare thyself even as I have prepared Mine own self" -- Give not thy pearls of price - unto them which would rend thee -- Ye shall be reminded of these Mine Words - when they come demanding of thee: "Give unto us of thy substance - that we might too be learned - that we might sup from thy cup"-- Let them learn that which is given unto them to learn: The Law: - "As ye are prepared - so shall ye receive"-- And they shall apply themself diligently - and be as the SERVANTS of the Lord - for this have I called them -- Yet is it said: "Many are Called - but few are chosen"-- Why? Why? I ask thee -- They are as ones unprepared for Mine Service - they choose to serve mammon --

While they say: "I am come that I might learn of thee"- I say they come with one hand in the till - one hand before their eyes - - they see not - neither do they give of themself that others be healed - that others be lifted up -- It is said: They give unto others to be seen of men - - they flount their learning before men - and call themself WISE! I say - they are fools indeed! They have not heard Mine Words - neither comprehended Mine Mission into the world of men -- They have "imaged a vain thing" - they have mocked Mine Sayings - and they have defiled the House of the Lord! Wherein have they saved a place for Me? Wherein have they given unto Me credit for being that which I Am?

They have paid the fiddler - and danced their merry tune - yet they pay Me no penny for Mine assistance --

I give freely and wisely - yet they ask of Me Proof! "Prove Thyself"- they ask of ME! and have I not? Yet do they come unto Me with clean hands - clean heart - willing to follow where I lead them?

= Pity =

O Man - fickle man - poor in Spirit art thou - frail of Spirit - - in need art thou!

I say - ye stand in need - therefore I send forth a Host to serve thee. Be ye alert - and seek the Light - and ye shall find it shall serve thee well -- So be it and Selah --

= Acceptance =

Sori Sori -- Be ye as one blest this day - and know ye that I come for the Good of All -- So be it that ye shall record that which I say unto thee - that they be blest -- So be it they which accept the Word shall be blest - - so let it be - as the Father hast willed it --

= Warning =

This is Mine Word unto them: There is but a little time in which to prepare thyself for the part which hast been kept for thee - and it behooves thee to be about thy preparation-- And for that is it said - that One shall be sent unto thee - that ye be quickened - that ye be prepared. For this is it said: "Be ye alert - and watchful - - Seek ye the Light"--

= The Touch =

For this are they sent forth - that ye be touched - - and ye shall first be as one touched - and quickened - and THEN ye shall Know that ye have been touched - and ye shall be alert unto the touch - - Then ye shall be as one prepared to receive that which is prepared for thee -- Accept that which they bring unto thee in Mine Name - - forget not that I bring them which are of the Host - for they bear Mine Seal - and they bear upon their head the Crown of the Sun - and they walk upright - as Sons of God - bearing upon their fore heads the Star of their Order - - they are not deceivers of darkness --

= Trust =

I have said: "Seek ye the Light - and it shall not be hidden from thee"- Yet - ye shall accept Mine Word - - and be ye as one prepared to follow where I lead thee - and turn not away from Me -- Know ye that I Am Sent that ye be delivered out of darkness -- So - let it be! - for I Am the Light - the Way - - I Am the Wayshower - Come follow where I lead thee - and be ye at Peace --

= Security =

This is Mine Word unto thee: Be ye not fearful - for I shall not forsake thee - I shall lead thee safely and surely - Mine hand shall uphold thee. Mine Shield shall be thine Shield -- Mine hand shall cover thee - and I shall anoint thee with sweet oil - and ye shall be as one comforted -- So let it be - - for this have I spoken -- So be it that I Am come - be ye as one blest to accept Me in the Name of the Father which hast Sent Me. So be it and Selah --

= The Blessing =

Sori Sori -- Be ye as one blest to receive Me - and ye shall bless others that they might in turn bless others -- Let us give unto others as we have received - and may it profit each and every one which shall receive this

Mine Word - for it is Sent forth that each one be blest -- This shall carry with it great blessings - they have but to receive it - for it is given unto Me to see some reaching out to take unto themself the Love sent forth, others rejecting it - for they have not the capacity to receive that which We send forth that they be blest --

= Foolish Ones =

They stand with their hands within their pockets and ask: "Why should I accept that which I know not?" "I am not of a mind to receive one whom I have not seen - or heard" -- Yet - wherein have they seen the one which hast betrayed himself - and them likewise? So be it they accept <u>his</u> word as <u>truth</u> - when he says: "I shall give unto thee the pleasures of the world - and fortunes untold - - I shall be unto thee the deliverer when ye serve me and follow me - doing mine bidding" --

The sweet honeyed tones of his - hast led them far afield - in search of happiness - so short lived - and it is but his trap - his plan to entrap them -- They seek the easy way - yet is it easy? I say - it is the long way round - it is the deceiver's way to ensnare thee - for there is no short-cut - no easy way - into the place of Mine abode --

= Neophyte =

It is a long - steep climb unto the Summit - - none to carry thee on their back -- Ye have to go thy own way - and be alert - and faint not - fear not -- Ask of no man his favor - - bless thyself - and be as one responsible for thy own failure or success - attainment --

= The Initiate =

Ye shall walk humbly - and be as one responsible for thy own part - and for thy own Self – So be it and Selah -- Ye shall be as one on whose head I place Mine hand - and I shall bless thee for thy loyalty - for thy progress shall be certain - and thy failure impossible - when ye have given of thyself unto the Way of the Lord - for it shall be the Way of Truth - Peace - Light -- So be it and Selah --

= The Sons of God & The Bastard Race =

Sori Sori -- This I would say unto thee at this time: The Host is but the TOOL within the Father's hand - by which His Work shall be accomplished - The Awakening - which shall be done according to the LAW -- The time hast come when We shall go forth as One Man - one body - and we shall go in strength - for no longer shall we go in single file -- We shall be as ONE - yet in strength - for we shall be undivided and we shall be as the Mighty Army - undefeated - we shall be as the UNDEFEATED! For this shall we be the Victor - we shall be Victorious - for we are about Our Father's Business - and this is the way in which He - The Father - would have us do His Work --

= Glory to God =

The WORK which He gives unto us shall be unto His Glory - unto Him all the Glory and the Praise - - so let it be -- For this do we say: Praise ye the Name of Solen Aum Solen --

Blest shall they be which are one with the Host, for <u>they</u> shall Know God - and they shall rejoice forever! So be it and Selah --

Let it be recorded - and let it go down in history - that which is said for it is for the Good of All -- While there are ones which will turn from the Light - there are ones yet unborn - which shall pay homage unto the Name of Solen Aum Solen - The Father of All Generations - born or unborn -- So be it that they shall sing His Praise in the place of His Abode - even before they are born of flesh - and they shall bring with them the Knowledge of their Father - their being One in Him - and their Eternal Being - their Inheritance --

= **Memory** =

They shall be as ones blest to remember their Heritage -- So let it be said that they which are yet unborn - shall sing His Praise as ones Knowingly - and as ones yet prepared to enter into flesh as men - - Men of Earth shall they come Knowingly - and they shall walk as man - Knowing themself to be Sons of God -- For this is it said: "Thy Kingdom Come" --

So shall it be in that day - when the "Sons of God" shall rejoice together as One in Him -- And there shall be Peace on Earth amongst men - for it shall come to pass - that the "Sons of God" shall inherit the Earth - and She - the Earth - shall no more be harassed by war and pillage -- So be it that She shall Know Peace - and She shall be delivered out of the hands of the fowler --

She shall no more be bound in the agony of labor - for She shall bring forth the Son which shall honor Her - as the Mother Earth - and they shall Glorify the Father -- It is said that the "Bastard" race shall be cast off - and no more shall She carry it upon Her back - for She shall be delivered of Her burden - and She shall go forth as the Mother of a New Race - the "Sons of God"-- And for this do we say: Be ye as one on whose shoulders rests Great responsibility - for it is now come when She is being purged - When She is being with child - and when She hast need of thy assistance - for each pain shall be borne with remembrance - and with the Knowledge of when - where - and Who give unto Her assistance in Her time of labor -- Unto these shall She give preference - - unto these shall She give footing - - unto these shall She give Peace - and comfort --

= The Jewel =

It is said - that the Earth shall be as a shining Orb within the firmament and it is So - for She is the One created to be Greatest amongst the ones within the Solar System -- She shall adorn the firmament with Her Light - and the joy shall know no bounds - it shall be as the Great Note of Harmony for which She was created - - No longer shall She send forth a discordant note - an undertone of discord - inharmony - a cry of distress!

= Deliverance Draweth Nigh =

Now it is come when She shall be delivered - and We as the "Host" shall be as midwife unto the Child which shall come forth - and establish the Kingdom of God upon the Earth --

= The Man Child =

Long hast "She" been in labor - long hast She labored to bring forth the "MAN CHILD"-- And many have spoken of - and about the "Man Child" - knowing not the meaning thereof -- Yet it is but the race of Man - which shall do honor unto the Father and Mother - and for this have We labored that it be done - that the race of Man might come into its own - its fullness - Come of Age - into maturity - into the Age of accountability - wherein it might receive its inheritance in full -- <u>Then</u> it shall be as one prepared to dwell in the House of the Lord forever -- So be it and Selah --

For this is it said: Be ye as one responsible -- For this is it said: Honor thy Father and thy Mother -- For this is it said: Be ye up and about thy Father's Business - - THAT HIS KINGDOM <u>BE ESTABLISHED UPON THE EARTH</u> - that ye be part of the Kingdom of God upon the Earth --

= The Ineffable Law =

Let it be understood - that in the Kingdom of God The Father - there are many Mansions - many places of abode - each one builded unto His Glory -- And there are untold numbers wherein there are beings of Great Majesty beyond thy reckoning - wherein they do dwell as Gods within their own right --

Yet ye of Earth shall be as ones prepared to dwell with them - in the same Order - and none escape the Law: "As ye are Prepared"-- This law is Ineffable - unchangeable -- This law is binding! and it behooves Me to say: "Prepare thyself for to receive thy inheritance in full"-- So be it and Selah

This is Mine Word unto thee at this hour -- So let it profit thee to give it unto them which are prepared to receive it -- So be it it shall profit them to receive it unto themself - and it shall be unto them Great Light -- So - let it be -- Amen - and Selah --

Recorded by Sister Thedra

= Acceptance of the Word =

Sori Sori -- Be ye as the hand of Me made manifest - and record this Mine Word - for them which will receive it unto themselves -- This I say - that ye might record it for their own good - the ones which have the mind to follow in the way I set before them --

First - it shall be given unto them to accept the Word - then they shall receive of Me - then they shall be as ones blest - for the Word precedes the manifestation -- The manifestation follows the Word - for I am the manifestation of the Word - and the Will of The Father made manifest --

This I would have thee Know:- that I Am come unto them which receive Me - and I am come in Spirit - - yet unto all which receive Me in Spirit - I shall manifest as the Son of God made flesh -- So be it and Selah --

= About the Coming =

This I shall do - and more - for I am come that they might Know - and be free of all their legirons which hast bound them - - bound them unto their opinions and ideas of - and about:- "The Coming"-- There hast been Great misunderstanding about "THE COMING"--

They have rejected Me - for the "coming" of their own vain imagining - They have misinterpreted the Word - they have misunderstood that which is recorded - for it hast lost its meaning - in its translations and interpretations by man --

= I am Come =

This is the Word I would give unto them: "This day - I Am Come - I am come in Spirit unto All which receive Me in Spirit - - I am Come in flesh - made manifest unto them which receive Me in Spirit"--

= In Spirit =

I am come even as I Am -- I Am that I Am - I Am Spirit! manifest as Spirit - unto them in Spirit -- And - unto them which walk with Me - IN SPIRIT - I manifest unto them in flesh - as flesh - as man - made flesh -- So be it - and Selah --

= Spirit in Flesh =

I Am the Will of Mine Father made flesh - made manifest -- So be it I come unto them which are prepared to receive ME and of ME - for they are <u>as</u> <u>the</u> <u>ones</u> <u>prepared</u> to receive ME -- <u>They</u> Know Me in Spirit - therefore they Know Me in flesh -- I am no stranger unto them - for they are with Me in SPIRIT --

This I would point out: I come as a "thief in the night" unto the ones which have not prepared to receive Me - and of Me -- It is said - that: "I shall go as I come "- - When? "they know not the hour"-- <u>These</u> shall be the ones which are not aware of Me - of Mine Presence--

= The will Made Flesh =

Let there be no misunderstanding about this - let the mystery be removed -- I am not of a mind to mystify thee -- I am not of a mind to confuse thee -- I speak plainly - and in thy own tongue -- I Am Come unto all which receive Me - in Truth and Light -- I am Come in flesh -

as one made manifest unto them which receive Me in Truth - and Light as the Word made flesh - - The Will - made manifest --

= The Needy =

This is the Word Ineffable made flesh - and none shall deny the Word and see God - for they are as yet unprepared - they are <u>not</u> prepared - they have not accepted Me - they have not Known ME - and they are in need of Light - they stand in NEED! they are in darkness/ bondage.

They are in the "mist" the "fog-mist" - they are befuddled - they neither see - hear - or know -- They are the ones which await some great Cosmic Shock - some Great Phenomenon - some Great Show of Splendor and power - that they be given proof of "The Coming" --

Have they not borne proof - have they not seen the Wonders - have they not heard the testimony of Mine: "The Coming" - have they not seen the Glory of the Lord - and testified thereto? -- Yet - these which have borne witness of the Glory of the Lord - are the ones which have seen - and Know --

= The Persecuted & The Persecutors =

Wherein have they been persecuted - stoned - blasphemed against - imprisoned - put to disrepute - cast out - and put to shame? I say unto the persecutors: "The Shame is thine - thy sins are upon thine head! Thine sins shall follow thee as thy shadow - and they shall be visited upon thy children's children - yea - their children - for it is given unto thee to be the forefathers of coming generations - therefore responsible for them -- That which ye leave as their inheritance - shall be unto thy glory - OR - unto thy undoing - So be it the LAW --

= Betray not Thyself =

It behooves thee to be up and about the Father's Business and leave no traps set - that <u>they</u> be entrapt - for therein shall ye be entrapt -- Let it be said: "By thy own traps shall ye be entrapt" --

This I would say unto the ones which deny Mine Words: Be ye as one on whose shoulders rests the responsibility of thy own decision - for to reject the <u>Word</u> - is to choose the way of darkness - - and to choose the way of darkness is to betray thyself --

Pity is he which betrays himself -- <u>The</u> <u>Word</u> is given unto thee as a Gift of The Father - yet to reject it is the way unto darkness and despair -- None cast them into the darkness - yet it is the way thou hast chosen - and ye shall find that ye have chosen thine own way - and the responsibility is thine alone. (To these which have rejected the Word).

Thou hast rejected the Light - the Truth -- Thou shall find that ye have chased the phantom which shall torment thee - ye shall find that ye have been deceived by the illusions which is created by the false - the deceiver - which hast given unto thee illusions of fear - of grandeur of great mysterious promises - and great speech - designed to impress thee - to ensnare thee --

Ye have followed the deceiver - therefore the responsibility is thine own - for have I NOT cried unto thee: "Come Out from amongst them and follow ye the Light"? Hast thou not the mind to Know the Light from the dark? Wherefore art thou given the mind to Know – to choose Wherein hast thou given unto Me credit for being that which I am? Wherein hast thou followed Me? Wherein hast thou given unto Me thine hand - and followed Me unto the end?

= Why Fear the Light? =

Thou hast been as One fearful of Me - of the Light - of that which I might reveal unto thee -- Thou hast feared the unknown - therefore ye walk in darkness - for the Light blinds thy eyes - and ye hide them - crying: "Show me NO MORE! I cannot bear it!"-- while I stand by as One prepared to lead thee into greater heights - safely - wisely - and gently - wherein ye might be delivered from all harm - all bondage - all darkness --

So be it I say: Shake off thy legirons - thy lethargy - and arise - come forth - and stand with Me - as one prepared to go where I lead thee - - for I have prepared a place for thee - wherein ye shall know as I know -- So be ye as one prepared to enter in - for none enter unprepared -- So be it and Selah -- I Am He which is Sent that there be Light - - so let it be --

= To the Instrument =

Be ye the Voice of Me - and say unto them in Mine Name: that I Am Come - tho they know it not -- I am Come – tho they know it not – I am come even as I shall go - while they sleep - knowing not that I

They have not seen - nor heard – Be it said: They shall first seek Me out - and they shall find that I Am come --

While they seek signs and wonders - they fail to find Me - for I am not come to comfort them - neither to satisfy their curiosity -- They shall seek Me in Truth and spirit -- They shall be as ones prepared to find - for they shall turn from their selfish way - and devote their time to service of the Whole --

= It is Said... =

Let it be understood that to serve Me is to serve Life - in Truth and Light -- There are ones which serve to be seen of man - to be praised of man - - and wherein is it said:- "Thy 'good' works are not sufficient"- for it is commanded of thee: Give of thine self that all be blest -- So be it that ye shall put aside thy selfishness - thy old concern for self - and be ye as the hand of God made manifest - - give unto Him credit for thy BEing - and unto Him all the Power and the Glory - asking nought for self sake -- Give thine self unto Him - wholehearted - and ye shall be acceptable in His sight -- So be it and Selah -- So be it that He hast set thee apart from all others - and He hast given unto thee a part which shall be part of the Whole --

Yet ye shall not fret for thy part - for He - The Father Knows the Plan - and thy part within it -- and thy part is but <u>one</u> part -- While all parts shall be as <u>part</u> of the Whole - only He - Knows what the fullness of the Whole is -- for this hast He given thee a part - that ye play thy part on the Stage of Earth - - while it is played for the most part on a darkened stage - it is said - that there shall be Light -- So let it blaze forth - that the final act shall be played in the Light - and to the Glory of the King of Kings! So let it be -- So be it – and Selah --

Sori Sori -- Be ye as one blest to receive Me and of Me - for I come that ye be blest -- So be it that ye shall be as one blest - for the time is come when I shall give unto thee that which I have kept for thee - and ye shall be glad to receive it -- Be ye as one on whose head I place My hand in Holy Benediction - and ye shall be blest –

= The Free Spirit =

By Mine own hand shall ye be blest -- Let it be recorded that which I say unto thee - that they might bear witness of Mine Words unto thee - So be it and Selah -- Ye shall stand upon the High Holy Mount with Me - and ye shall rejoice that the time is come when ye have been given the part which is fortuned unto thee -- So be it that I speak as One Knowing -- I Know - for I see as ye cannot see - - yet ye have seen - ye have come unto Me - ye have stood with Me in the hours of thy unknowing - - for while thy body hast slept - thy Spirit in its flight - hast come as one free to bear witness of thine own fortune - thine own part -- And for this have ye been brot into the place wherein I am - - ye have been fortuned to come into the place wherein I am - - and ye shall come and go as ye come - and ye shall remember that which ye have seen - heard and done - that which hast been said - and ye shall return and bear witness of that which ye have seen - heard - and done -- So be it and Selah --

* * *

Sori Sori -- By Mine own hand shall ye be led into fields afar - and ye shall have no fear - for I shall be with thee unto the end -- So be it and Selah --

Behold ye the Glory of the Lord -- Be ye as one prepared to behold the Glory of the Lord -- Be ye as one prepared to go where I lead thee. So be it I shall lead thee gently - and safely -- So be it and Selah --

Be ye as one on whose head I shall place Mine hand in Holy benediction - and I shall bless thee - and I shall give unto thee a part which shall bless thee -- Ye shall be blest as I have been -- So be it and Selah --

By the Word shall ye be blest - by the Word shall others be blest -- Ye shall give it unto them which ask for Light - and they shall bear witness of the Word - for it is for them which seek the Light --

= The Host =

They which seek shall find - and be blest to Know they have found it - So be it and Selah --

Mine <u>Word</u> I would give unto them -- This is that which I would send forth as a Mighty Power -- There is a Host which hast gone forth that there be Light in the world of man -- The Host shall pass over them and touch them - - they shall feel the touch - and be healed of their blindness/ their unbelief -- They shall hear and Know - for it is now come when the Host hast gone forth to do a Mighty Work -- The Work which is allotted unto them is <u>Mine</u> <u>Work</u> - for I have given unto them the Power and the Authority - to go forth in Mine Name - and they shall <u>Not</u> fail - for theirs is a mission of Mercy --

= The Council =

They have prepared long for this hour - when they might go forth - and be the hand and foot of the Great and Mighty Council -- They go forth with the consent of the Council - and the Council is the Will of The Father manifest --

The Council sits in Counsel - for the purpose of bringing forth the fulfillment of the Law -- The Council is the Law giver - the Law is the

Will of The Father - for He Wills it - and it is Law - for all things are done according to Law --

= Transgression & Repentance =

The Law - <u>is</u> the <u>Law</u> - and none escape it - - all things come under the Law - for wherein a law is transgressed - it brings great stress - great pain - sorrow -- The transgressor pays for his transgression - and atones for it by his own actions - by his turning from his transgressions - and being as one filled with Love of righteousness - - and from that moment of his turning from his transgressions - he remembers no more them - he gives no thot unto them - for his transgressions are remembered no more -- He gives all his energy - himself - wholly unto the Light - the way of right-eousness - and he walks in the Light - looking not backward -- He looks strait ahead - walks upright - which way his Crown tilts not -- He knows himself to be a servant of the Living God, he gives of himself that others might see his light - and walk in his footsteps -- So be it he too becomes a Light bearer --

= The Ones Called =

There are ones which are called - and they hear not -- There are ones which hear and answer not - there are ones which answer and come not. There are ones which are called - which answer - they come and are received - and these are as the ones prepared - for they have complied with the law - they have surrendered themself - they have said: "Father Thy Will be done in me - by me - and thru me - let <u>it</u> BE!"-- So be it these I shall bless - these I can and do give a part which shall profit them -- They shall know no sorrow - they shall be delivered out of darkness - and suffering -- So be it - and Selah --

Bear ye in mind:- I am come into the WORLD OF MAN - for the good of all - yet not <u>All</u> receive Me - they seek the dark places - they turn from Me - they sneer at Mine <u>Word</u> - they mock Me - persecute Mine Servants - and make a mockery of the Word -- They give no credence unto the WORD - they become the "sinners"-- Therefore it is said: Turn from thy own way - and follow the path of righteousness - - so be it that I call unto them: "Come - Come ye out from among them" and it behooves Me to say again - and again: "Come" - for they which have not heard Mine Voice <u>shall</u> hear - and they which come shall be blest -- So be it and Selah –

= They that Ask for the Latest Messages =

Sori Sori -- This is Mine Word unto them which ask: "What is the latest?"--

Tell them that the latest is yet to be said - yet to be told - for the latest hast not yet been revealed --

There is no place wherein the Word shall be hidden - for it shall be made manifest before their eyes -- While they see in part only - they know not that which they see - for they are as the blind - looking for the events which are yet to come --

They have been told thus and so shall occur - and they wait with expectancy for the worst - - while I say: They shall wait with expectancy for the Greatest event known unto man --

For the time is come when the Host shall go forth in such power - as man hast not known - and they shall begin to awaken - - as such they shall be called out of their beds - and they shall bestir themself --

Therefore they shall be as one which has been touched/ quickened/ and stirred -- They shall pick up their feet and move - for they shall know that they have been touched --

They shall be as ones come alive - and they shall be aware of that which goes on about them - and they shall walk Knowingly --

For this hast the Host gone forth - that they be brot out of darkness, out of bondage -- So let it be - - and for this have I spoken -- So be it and Selah --

SYMBOLS OF THE WORD

Sori Sori -- By Mine own hand shall ye be led into the place wherein I am - and ye shall stand with Me upon Mine High Holy Mount - and Know ye that I am the One Sent to bring thee out -- So be it - and Selah.

This is the Word which I give unto thee at this hour: Prepare thyself for the next part which I shall give unto thee this day -- So be it it shall be for them which seek the Light which I Am --

= Temporary Freedom =

Sori Sori -- The Word which I would give unto thee at this hour is - the Word which hast been sent forth in the hours of thy sleep -- That which is given unto thee while thou art free of the physical body - is that which is Greater than the written word - which is but the symbol of the Word as it is given unto thee while thou art free of the dense body -- While it is but temporary that ye are free - it is for the most part like unto the permanent freedom - which is after thou hast finished with the physical/ dense body --

This is but the poor part of "UN"- for it is given unto thee to see faintly - that which lies ahead of thee - and it is but the beginning of thy seeing - and thy Knowing --

They which have put aside the dense body of flesh - are free of it - yet some there be which know it not -- Some there be which are prepared to leave it - and they walk free from the senses of the dense body - without any legiron - any fetters which bind them unto it - - they are prepared to soar unto heights unknown - they go as ones free - they have prepared themself to go where I go - they have given unto Me credit for being that which I Am -- Therefore I lead them safely and gently - wherein they shall abide with Me - - and together We journey out into the regions far - and wide --Without any fear - they follow where I lead them --

They know Me for that which I Am - and they give unto Me credit for Knowing that which I do - and shall do - - for they are as ones prepared to go where I go -- So be it these shall be blest as I have been blest -- So be it and Selah --

= Miracles =

Hear ye Me in this: I am now come into the dense world of man - that all might Come - All might be delivered - yet I see them fearful - awaiting that day wherein great and miraculous things shall happen -- Wherein hast there not been great happenings - wherein hast there been a day that I have not given unto them miracles? (Things they call miracles - <u>so soon forgotten</u>)--

= Impatience =

They see - and forget - they ask - and wait not - they ask and fear to receive -- They fear - therefore they look not - they wait not - for they are demanding - they fret for the worldly things - they are not at Peace.

They are not at Peace - - within themself they are at war - they are divided within themself - they are as the house divided -- They ask - and fear they have not been heard - - they ask and wait not --

The know not there is a time of fulfillment - a time of reaping a time for bringing in --

They are prone to rush headlong into the on-rush - and bring upon themself great pressure - great stress - and for this they agonize - and cry out: "How Long Lord - How Long?"

So be it I say unto them: "Be ye at peace - peace be established within thee - and be ye as one prepared to see - and hear - that which I do - and say unto thee - and ye shall be as one prepared for a greater work -- So be it - for I have need of thee"--

Now ye shall stand in need - and ye shall be as one prepared to receive that which ye need -- For this hast the Host gone forth - that thy needs be filled - that ye might be prepared to go where I go -- So be it and Selah --

Nowhere have I said the word which shall deny thee thy heritage - thy inheritance -- No place have I said - ye shall not inherit the Kingdom of God -- Yet I <u>have</u> <u>said</u>: "Ye shall first prepare thyself to receive - so be it the Law"-- So let it be as thou art prepared - - for this is it said: I Am Come that ye be prepared - - I am come that ye have understanding of the LAW -- So be it I am now prepared to give unto thee according to thy capacity to receive -- So be it and Selah --

= Pass Ye In =

Sori Sori -- I come in the Glory of the Light which I Am -- I come in the Light which I Am -- I am come that ye be prepared to enter into the Inner Chamber -- I come that ye be prepared for the Feast - for the Wedding Feast -- I come that ye might drink of the Cup which I proffer thee -- therefore I proffer thee the Cup of Crystal Water - the water of Life - Eternal Life --

= The Inner Chamber =

This is the Gift giver unto all which enter into the Inner Chamber - the Holy of Holies - the Inner Temple -- This is the Gift of the Immortal One - the One Which holds within His Hand the Power to give Life - and to take as He hast given --

= The Passport =

It is said: Thy passport is in order -- I say unto thee: Pass ye in - - I say unto thee: "Pass ye in" - and thou hast heard Me - thou hast turned the Key - and the door stands a jar before thee - - yet thy foot is but upon the threshold - and it shall not slip - for I am with thee that it slip not - I shall secure thy faltering foot - for thou hast been obedient- unto Mine touch - thou hast followed where I have led thee - and thou hast asked nought save to serve -- Thou hast not given unto Me the puny part of thyself -- Thou hast served Me whole-heartedly - willingly - without thot of reward -- Now I say unto thee: Enter ye in - and be ye as one on whose head I place Mine hand in Holy Benediction - - and I now speak the Word: "Pass ye in" --

So be it that I Know thee - and I have set Mine Seal upon thee - and it shall serve thee well - for by the Seal which I place upon thee shall ye be Known - by thy Light shall ye be Known in thy own right - for by thine dedication - obedience - and application of the law hast thy Victory been won - - I say: "been won" - for We see it as won - for we know thee for that which thou art - and not as <u>they</u> see thee -- They Know thee not - they see thee not - they understand not that which they see -- So be it that they are poor of Spirit/ blind art they for they have not been quickened - - they have not been as ones responsive unto the Word - they have not been quickened unto Mine touch --

= The Hosts' Mission =

For the quickening - I have sent forth the Host - which shall pass amongst them and touch them - and they shall begin to stir -- They shall be quickened - and they shall know the <u>touch</u> - and respond unto it -- So be it THESE shall be brot out from amongst them - and they shall be as ones prepared to join the "Host" - and then - they in turn shall go forth and seek the ones which are yet in the places wherein they labor for bread - and wherein they sleep the sleep of the dead -- They which have joined the Mighty Host - shall be as <u>Mine</u> hand - they shall have the power and authority to speak unto them in their own tongue - their own words - which shall be understandable unto them --

And they shall be blest to hear - and understand - for the <u>next of kin</u> shall go unto the "next of kin" - and they shall show themself- and be received as a kinsman - as one known and acceptable -- Neighbor shall go to neighbor - friend unto friend - father to son - to daughter - - mother to son - to daughter - - sister to brother - brother to sister - brother to brother -- and they shall not be as ones fearful - for they shall be led gently and firmly --

Many there be which shall hear and see - and come forth as ones prepared for their deliverance -- Such be Mine Word unto thee this hour record ye the hour - and let it go on record - for the hour shall be as the hour - the day shall be as the day - the year as the year -- Yet it is said: There is no time - only NOW -- It is for this that I say unto thee: "This is the time of thy awakening - - the time of thy awakening is NOW -- Come ye forth - and be ye as one prepared - for <u>this</u> is the time of thy Calling - - <u>hear ye Me NOW</u>"--

Blest is he which hears Me - and responds unto Me NOW - - wait ye for another - and be ye as one found wanting! - Be ye alert - for I have said unto thee: "There are none so sad as he which betrays himself"- so be it a Truth -- Let it suffice thee that I am come that ye be delivered out of bondage-- So be it and Selah --

Ye- shall find that I am not a traitor - for I shall not mislead thee -- I shall be true unto Mineself/ Mine trust - for I am Sent of Mine Father that there be Light in the World of Men -- So let it be as He hast Willed it -- Amen and Selah.

= The Introduction =

Sori Sori-- I bring One unto thee which hast within his hand the power and the authority to speak in Mine Name - and for this I say unto thee: Receive him in Mine Name - - so let it profit thee -- So be it and Selah.

This I would say unto thee: I am come for the purpose of adding Mine Light unto thine - and it is for this that I speak -- Blest shall ye be to receive Me - and blest shall I be that ye receive Me - for we shall do a work which is given unto us of the Great and Mighty One - - and it shall be for the upliftment of mankind - for the Good of mankind -- So be it and Selah --

There are many prepared to speak - yet for this shall they be brot by the One known as Sananda - the "Doorkeeper" - for He shall stand Sentinel that none pass unprepared - that none pass which are not of the Light --

This is the part which we shall be given: - that of bringing Light - of bringing forth understanding between the worlds seen and unseen by man --

For this I say unto thee: The "unseen" shall become seen - and the seen shall become unseen - and there shall be greater knowledge of the unseen - for the unseen shall become thy reality - - while that which now seems real shall become as the unseen - and be as the passing of a shadow --

That which man hast held so close and dear unto himself as possessions - as <u>things</u> - he shall come to know - are but the poor part of reality - the transient part of matter which is perishable - and passes into the unseen from which it came -- The <u>things</u> which man hast called <u>his</u> <u>own</u> - are but the forms of thot made manifest - and which shall pass as the thot which created the form -- So be it that the creation of man hast tormented him - and brot about his downfall - - for this does he cry out for relief from his own creation--

= Hideous Thot Forms =

Man hast created in his own image - he hast created that which now torments him -- His own creation now stands as hideous monsters to devour him -- He now stands face to face with his monsters - he fears them! and knows not which way to run - - he knows no escape - therefore I say: He stands face to face with his monsters --

= Manifestation =

He hast imaged vain imagings - and he hast brot forth his GIGANTIC MONSTERS - which are but his own downfall -- He hast labored long to bring these to life - giving them power over him - giving them power to destroy his Peace of Mind -- His own soul he hast sold for a poor penny - - now he cries out for help and he shall be heard - - for this am I now come - that Man be called out of his place of iniquity - out of his place of abode - - that he be as one prepared for the next part which he is to play in the Great Drama of the Age --

= The Great Drama =

For the Greatest Drama of All Ages is now being played upon the Stage of time - -

    Now - I say! NOW it is being played - yet to an audience which are blind unto the point of seeing nothing - not seeing the Light which is hidden from their sight - the Veil being heavy - the light obscure - their eyes blinded by their own hands - which they hold before them -- The Light hidden by their hand - shines as the Sun - yet they see not the Light - for they fear to look - they fear the Light ---

    They are as the Actors within this Great Drama - yet they know not their lines - they know not the Director - neither do they know they have written their own part within this <u>Drama</u> --

    Now it is come when they shall be caught up short - and they shall be given the next part - which they shall play unto the same world - - the same part which they have forgotten -- They shall be as ones rehearsing the "same old play"- and the lines shall be familiar unto them, yet they shall not remember the plot - only their own lines --

= Akasha =

Yet it is necessary that they know well their part - for they shall be as part of the Great Play -- While it is played for the most part on the darkened Stage - they shall be as ones prepared to stand face to face with the entire Company and all parts shall fit together and be as one part -- As each shall put himself into his own part - and <u>play it well.</u> He shall be as the one prepared to give of himself for the good of All - which shall profit the Whole --

And none shall be without "Direction" for the Director Knows each and all parts - and He hast within His hand "The Book"- and He Knows wherein all the parts are written - and wherein all the players belong - and what shall be their places - - and their parts shall be as One part within the Whole -- <u>This</u> He sees and Knows aforehand - therefore He moves amongst them - and gives unto them as they are prepared to receive -- So be it that He withholds not that which is profitable unto them --

He is the Director - and He hast the knowledge of all the parts and participants - their qualifications - and where to find them -- So be it and Selah -- Ye shall return at a later hour - and we shall continue this discourse of preparedness --

Recorded by Sister Thedra

= Attainment =

Sori Sori -- Be ye the hand of Me - and record that which I say unto thee - that they might bear witness of this - Mine Word for them --

They - which seek the Light shall find - and they shall be as ones prepared for the Greater part -- These which are prepared shall be brot into the Inner Temple - wherein All Mysteries shall be revealed - and wherein there are NO mysteries --

= The Mysteries =

The Mysteries - are mysteries for thy unknowing -- When ye know - there no longer remains a mystery -- This is the way of the novice - - the mysteries are for him - for he knows not -- Yet he seeks to know - he seeks to find -- While many do weary of their search - many do attain such knowledge as fits them for greater parts - Greater Service --

= Action =

The first step unto knowledge is desire - desire leads to action - action leads to attainment - attainment leads to Wisdom - and therein is the <u>Secret</u> of Attainment --

So be it that I am come that each and every one attain unto Wisdom for none shall be given the Key of attainment without action - without preparation - - and the preparation is the Key to Attainment - - Attainment is the result of preparation -- So be it and Selah --

= Responsibility =

Think ye not that there is an easy - short way to attainment - for it is by Action - preparation - application of the law - that ye grow in Grace - that ye grow to maturity - that ye become accountable for the part which hast been allotted unto to thee -- It is said: Ye shall be as one responsible for thine part - it is So -- So let it be - and let it profit thee - for it is the way of Attainment --

= Reward =

The reward follows the preparation - the attainment is the reward- - for thine attainment is the Crowning Glory - for it is thine own- and no man shall rob thee of that which thou hast earned by thy own effort -- that which thou hast labored for - is thine own by law -- Self-acquired is the Wisdom of the wise - - the experience of the neophyte shall profit him, the Wisdom of the Gods shall be his - when he hast attained to his fullness - his inheritance – For it is said that as ye are prepared - so shall ye receive – So be it and Selah --

= Faithfulness =

For this is it said: "Turn not aside - come unto Me – for I go before thee that ye might not fail - - Come - Come follow Me - and I shall be unto thee thy Shield and thy Buckler"-- So be it and Selah --

= Simplicity =

While many tire of the Way I set before them - it is said: Fear not - turn not to the left or to the right - for Mine is the strait and narrow Way - it is the safe and sane Way-- Practical is Mine Way - for I give unto thee no complicated formulas - creeds - dogmas - no misleading doctrine -- I say: "Come - and I shall lead thee"-- This is Mine Way: - simplicity - Simplicity!- and it shall not be given unto Me to give unto thee any complicated formulas - to confuse thee or deter thee from thy course - So be it I am a Simple Man - and I ask not of thee that I am not -- I am about Mine Father's Business - therefore I say unto thee: "Be ye about the Father's Business - even as I Am"--

= The Path =

There is but One Way unto the Father's House - that is the Way in which I lead thee - the "Path of righteousness"- and that / this path - leads unto Him -- So be it no other shall ye find - - so let Mine Way be thine - and thy freedom is assured thee --

= The Reward =

Be ye as one prepared to enter in - so be it thy reward - thy inheritance. So let it profit thee to hear Me - and to receive of Me - that which I have for thee -- So be it I have kept for thee a goodly fortune –.

= The Admonition =

Sori Sori -- Hear Me in this - there is much to be done - and it behooves Me to say: It is time to rest thyself - and profit thereby -- Fear not for little things - - be ye as one prepared to do that which I give unto thee to do - so let it profit thee -- Be ye blest to hear Me this day - and give unto Me credit for being wise - - and Know that which I say unto thee.- So be it and Selah --

= Porter Speaks =

Sori Sori -- Be ye as one blest to receive Me and of Me - for I come in the Name of the Mighty Council - - and it is for thy sake that I come - I come that ye be blest -- So be it that I give unto thee that which shall profit thee --

Ye shall be as one on whose head I place Mine hand in Holy Benediction - and ye shall accept that which I have for thee - in the Name of Him Which hast Sent Me --

This I would say unto thee: It is given unto Me to Know thee - and to bear witness of thee -- Now ye shall come into the place wherein I am as one prepared -- Ye shall return unto them - and bear witness of that which ye SEE and DO - that which ye have <u>done</u> and seen -- So be it it shall profit them to learn of thee - and that which ye bring unto them -- Be ye blest of Me this hour - and return at another hour - for further concourse - further discourse -- So be it profitable unto thee --

= The Time? "Now"! =

While it is for the good of all that I speak - I say unto thee: Ye shall be blest to receive Me and of Me - for the time is come when we shall begin a Work which shall bring much Light unto the people now in flesh - now incarnated in flesh as man --

This is the way in which we shall move: - in power - with the law as the Fortress - and the Light as the Flame -- The Light shall burn away all the dross - all that which obstructs the way - the way before us - for we shall surmount all barriers - by the Light --

The Light shall be our tool - our weapon - and our garments shall be as the Light - and nothing shall stay us - for we shall go forth as a Force of Light = Light Force = and the darkness shall disappear before the Light -- So be it that the Force of Light shall sweep over the land - the Sea - and the people thereof shall be as ones prepared - they shall be as ones caught up in the Forces - which shall sweep the land - and they shall be brot out of their places of abode - as ones prepared for their new places of abode-

Some - shall find they have betrayed themself - these shall cry out in their betrayal - for help - assistance - for Mercy -- while some shall find their reward within the place wherein there is No Sorrow - no fear no want -- These shall be the ones which have obeyed the Call - and been unto themself true -- So be it that each shall find his rightful place the place for which he hast prepared himself - - so be it the law - and as he is prepared - so shall he receive --

= Present Time =

This is the time for Me to say: Time is of the essence - and time shall be when they shall remember that which is said - and they shall be as ones reminded of these Mine Words -- For this do I speak - that they be reminded -- So be it that I come from afar - that I might add Mine own energy - Mine Light unto the Host which hast gone forth for to awaken a sad and sorrowful world --

= Mastery =

By <u>Mine own Light</u> shall I find Mine way - and by Mine own way - shall I return unto Mine abiding place -- And this I would have thee Know: I am not One of thine Order - - I am of another Order - far removed from thine own - and not One of thine Order hast been of Mine for there is no turning back - when one becomes of Mine Order -- In other words - the two Orders are far removed - and none which are of Mine Order shall ever desert into dense flesh - or dense matter -- None have taken upon themselves flesh - as man - for it is not necessary that we do so --

It is not expedient - for the Greater part lies before the Order of Man and we have not the desire or necessity - to fall below Our Estate - which is far advanced - farther than man -- And yet it is the Greatest which thou hast attained - - yet greater shall he attain - for his progress is the Will of The Father Which hast begotten thee -- He is The Father of All - yet it is said: "It hast not been shown unto thee - what ye shall become "--

= Children of Earth =

It is said: "Man hast not come into his fullness - his inheritance" - it is truly so -- So be it and Selah --

= Credit Where Credit is Due =

I bow unto the Father - and I give unto Him All the Glory and the Praise yet He hast given unto Me passport into the World of Man - that I might assist at this moment of Her Initiation - and in the time of Her trial -- I say: "Her time of trial" - for She is on trial --

= Sponsors =

I come that I might stand Sponsor for Her - that I might bear witness of Her - and assist in the time of sore need --

This is the Word I would give unto thee at this hour -- Be ye blest to accept Me and to Know Me - and We shall do a Mighty Work - for it is the hour long awaited - - long awaited! - when the help cometh in Great Power - Great Strength - fully armed and prepared -- For this do I say - We are One - One in Mind - One in Power - One in Purpose --

Stand ye up and be counted - - so shall it profit thee --

= The Perfect Plan =

Sori Sori -- The hour hast struck when again We come unto this Altar for this communication - this meeting - when I might give unto thee this Word - which shall be given unto them which are prepared to receive it --

It is Mine part to say unto them:- that the way is now open before them - that they might enter into the place wherein I Am - and wherein there is Peace - Perfect Peace --

This is the Perfect Plan - - this is the part which is given unto Me: - to Come unto thee - that ye be as Mine hand made manifest unto them their part to accept that which is given unto thee for them - - then I shall touch them which receive it unto themself - - these I shall anoint - with the Holy Spirit - these I shall bless and give unto them - as they are prepared to receive -- So be it and Selah --

It is given unto thee to be Mine Voice unto them -- Yet I shall touch them - and then they shall be as ones quickened unto Mine touch -- Then - they shall awaken unto Me - and hear Mine Voice -- They shall Know Mine Voice and respond unto it -- So be it and Selah --

= Pioneer/ Anchor Man =

Open up ye the door - that I might enter into the world of men -- Open up the ears of men - that they might hear Me - that I might come in and give unto them that which I have for them -- So let it profit thee to be the Pioneer - the Gate Keeper unto them/ unto Me - - for I say: Ye shall open the way for Mine entrance into the World of Men -- And I shall enter in - and it is said in thy world: Be ye the "Anchor Man"- and let the anchor be deep and steady - for I shall go forth as One prepared to do a New Work amongst them - and they shall be moved - they shall Act - and accomplish a New thing - they shall do a New thing --

It is said: God shall accomplish His Strange Act - in the time of His Choosing -- It is now come when He shall accomplish this "Strange Act" -- Yet "they" shall not know the wherefore of His Working - - His hand shall move - and they shall be as ones blind unto the movement thereof -- While they shall See the results thereof - they shall be part of the movement - and know that they are moved -- They shall be glad they are so moved - for they shall come to Know that they are directed in the way in which they shall go --

= The Green Nuts =

While there are many which shall know not - for they are as the ones which shall turn from the Light - and choose the way of darkness -- These shall be as ones put in their place - and they shall await another day --

= The Accounting =

The ones that are prepared - shall be directed into the place wherein they shall receive their enua - and wherein they shall be prepared to stand before the High Tribunal and give an account of themself --

These shall be as ones tried - tested - and found worthy to enter into the Inner Chamber - wherein they shall receive of the Tribunal that which is their inheritance - their reward - - their reward having been earned thru and by their own effort - - and by their own desire have they prepared themself to enter in -- So be it that these shall stand as Sentinels upon the High Holy Mount with Him which hast given unto Me passport unto thee --

So be it that these shall be as ones blest to be part of the Great Host - which shall comprise the Greater Light - which shall draw forth the ones which are yet in darkness - for in the time to come they shall awaken unto the Light - - then they shall be as ones awake and strengthened - that they might endure the Light -- Then they shall be as the ones which can stand of their own strength - and come forth as ones prepared --

= The Safe & Sure Way =

There shall be no abortions - no pollutions - no pillage -- "No abortion" I say - for we shall not abort the sleepers - - they shall develop and come forth in due season - - therefore it is said: A place is prepared for them - and they shall sleep until they awaken of their own accord --

While it is said - that we go forth that they be awakened - I say: Some sleepeth lightly - and these shall awaken at the Sound of the first Touch - the first "Trumpet"-- Some shall wait the second - some the third - and each shall be given as he is prepared to receive - each shall find his place to serve - and serve he shall - in his capacity -- So be it and Selah --

For this do we come - that each be served - that they be prepared for greater service - and for the Greater Glory -- This is Mine Word unto thee at this hour --

= Instructions =

Now ye shall place this within the book with the other records - and it shall stand as the <u>Word</u> which shall be fulfilled unto the Glory of Solen Aum Solen which hast been unto Me the Light - the Life which I Am. So be it and Selah --

Praise ye His Name - and Sanctify His Presence -- Sanctify the Name amongst men - - Sanctify the Name of Thedra amongst men - that the Name be as the part of Light - which shall stand Immortal for all time - - and which shall be as a Tribute unto women -- Sanctify the time - by doing that which is given unto thee to do -- Let the day - the year - the hour be recorded on the pages of history - when man first received the Word of the Lord of Lords - when the Word went forth - when the Host went forth in great number --

Let them remember the time - and mark it well - - this is "The day of awakening - and ye shall see them stir as NEVER before - for this rustle of the winds - foretell the great awakening-- So bear ye in mind the time is at hand - when they shall come forth as ones alert - <u>Awake</u> - and be as ones prepared for the "Greater Part" -- So be it as the Father hast Willed it - Amen - and Selah --

To The Mighty Council:-

Which of these go into the book?

These are given for the book as they are received - none to be omitted - for this time -- Yet the book shall be for the most part ignored by the mass - - while the ones which are prepared shall find meat within that which now seems without merit unto thee -- So be it We see them which shall be enligtened by the Word as it is given unto thee -- So be it that it shall profit them to find comfort and Light within these pages for they shall endure with time - for time shall enhance them to the generations yet unborn -- So be it and Selah --

= Spirit Speaketh unto Spirit =

Sori Sori -- For this hour let us consider well the time - for it is now come when many have begun to stir - they question - and for the most part seek the answers - in the place wherein there is much darkness --

They ask of men who have not the answers -- while it is given unto them to be as ones walking in darkness - seeing not --

These who question - inquiring of men - shall seek the Light - they shall ask of the ones of Light - for therein they shall find their answers, therein shall they be enlightened --

The ones which seek the Light shall be enlightened of the ones of Light - and they shall give unto them as it is wise and prudent - - they shall receive according to their capacity -- So be it and Selah --

Now ye shall be as one blest to receive in greater measure - for thou hast been as one alert - as one trust worthy - and no place hast thou been found wanting -- So be it that ye shall stand fast - and ye shall bear witness of Me - and that which I say unto thee - and ye shall be glad for thy preparation --

For this day let us speak of the things which are to be done -- The first shall be a recognition of the Host which hast gone forth that there be Light within the world of men--

Then ye shall be as one responsive unto them which come unto thee and ye shall be as one prepared to receive them in the Name of the Father Which hast Sent them forth --

Then ye shall give unto them assistance - and they shall assist thee and it shall be as a meeting of the Waters - a blending - and a coming together - that the way of the Lord be made strait before them which seek the Light --

They which seek the Light shall be found - protected - brot out of bondage - they shall be as ones alert - and know the true from the false for they shall Know - they shall not be misled - and they shall be glad for their preparation and protection --

Ye shall stand as Sentinel for some of them which come unto thee and ye shall be as their Shield and Buckler - for it is so decreed - that ye be as one prepared for this part --

Now ye shall bear witness of these Mine Words - and ye shall Know that which I say unto thee -- So be it and Selah --

Wait not for thine inheritance in full - for it is so given unto thee - the Gifts which are necessary for this present day - for this work now - which is the Now - the present time - the NOW - THIS DAY -- wait not for another --

Be ye as one alert - and remember that which I say unto thee - - it shall profit thee -- So be it and Selah --

= Sananda Raises His Voice Against the Enemy =

Sori Sori -- Be ye as Mine Voice unto them which await this Word - and let it be recorded - that it might go into the record for them which follow thee --

This I would have them Know: The way of the Lord is strait and narrow - and it is the safe way - - there are no traps - set for thy foot - none to ensnare thee -- There is no place wherein ye shall find the places for thy comfort - which is designed to ensnare thee --

= Traps =

While the great wide road of destruction is set with jeweled lights - with the traps designed for thy foot - which fit thy foot - - and it is given unto Me to see them put their foot into them - to see if they fit - for they believe Me not -- They set their own traps - that others be entrapt - - they are not alone! there are many which set themself the task of designing such traps - - these are therefore fashioning for themself their own --

It is said: "By their own traps shall they be entrapt"- and it is so -- It is said: "They shall drink of the bitter cup they brew for their fellowmen"- it is a truth -- So be it that I come that they might not be ensnared unawares --

So be it that I now say: Be ye aware of their snares - for some are clever - some are as the posy wherein the serpent lurks - - and it is the cleverness of the false one which deceives them which are so foolish as to seek the wide and glamorous way - the popular way - which is crowded with the populace - - the populace which know not that they travel the highway to destruction --

= The Disciple =

The one which walks alone with surety - head high - upon the strait and narrow way - is the one which has heard Mine Voice and answered it - and the one which hast come forth as the one prepared to go where I lead him --

This is the one which shall be blest of Me and by Me - for I can reach him - and give unto him of the Good Gifts which shall be unto him profitable --

= The Enemy Advertizes =

While the one on the wide - glittered road of destruction - hears nought except the din of their own making - and they see nought save the tinsel and glimmer of their own carefully laid traps - - these beckon unto them: "Come - partake of the pleasures - come - see what is given for thy own pleasure - look - see - what we have provided for thy entertainment - this is the greatest place - for have we not a more tempting feature - have we not provided human flesh for our offering? Have we not given unto thee human sacrifice - that ye be pleased? Come partake of these pleasures!!!"--

= Sananda's Cry =

O - Man of Earth! Hear ye Me this day! HEAR YE ME - I say!!

I raise Mine Voice in indignation! I speak with a loud Voice - I raise Mine Voice against thee - for it is given unto Me to see thee - as the dragon - encamped in flesh -- I see thee as devils ensouled in flesh -- I say: I see thee as ones going down unto eternal "damnation"- for thou art unaware of the "pit"-- I speak of the pit - wisely - Knowingly - for I see the gaping pit before thee - at the end of the wide hiway on which ye travel --

= Warning =

I say: Turn ye quickly - look - see - be ye as ones thotful of Mine Words and take ye heed - for I Am the One Sent that ye be warned - that ye be told - that ye be delivered -- Yet ye shall hear Me - ye shall listen unto Me - - heed that which I say - and come of thy own accord - - so let it be as ye will -- I shall not be responsible for thy failure - for I shall not betray Mine own Self - nor Mine trust --

I say: Fashion no legirons for thyself - no traps to entrap thyself - and be ye as one responsible for thine own salvation - for I have gone before thee to prepare the way for thee - and ye have but to follow where I lead thee -- So be it it shall profit thee to follow Me -

= Hast Thou Heard Me? =

I offer unto thee no temptations - no tinsel - no glamorous trappings - - I offer thee Salvation - Eternal Salvation - Eternal Freedom - - Hast thou heard Me?

I give unto thee the Law - ye have but to obey it - and be spared the fate of destruction - the fate worse than death!

Let it be said - that there are ones which shall deny Mine Word - and give unto another credit for them - - yet be it Known that I am not a cringing - poor priest - I Am Come in Power - in Glory - in the Name of Mine Father -- I walk with sure foot - I step not into the hole - I put not Mine foot into their traps --

= To them that Hath Ears =

I come with a loud cry: "LOOK SEE - See the traps set to ensnare thee to destroy thee" - these are set by <u>Mine</u> enemy - Mine enemies -- I come with raised Voice against <u>them</u> - that ye be spared -- I cry out unto thee that ye might be aware of thine own part - of thine own downward flight saying: "TURN! Turn ye unto the Light - for destruction lieth ahead of thee! COME - Come unto ME - and I shall lead thee safely"--

These that come - that come out from among them - shall be brot out - and they shall be as ones prepared for the Greater part -- So be it and Selah --

= Self Responsibility =

I have spoken - in language simple and sanely - I have pointed Mine finger at Mine enemy - - I have raised Mine Voice against him - I have declared him Mine enemy - and he hast heard Me - and he hast given no ground -- Now I ask of thee: Follow him not - give unto him no allegiance - - no part shall ye have with him --

Ye shall be as one on whose shoulders rests the responsibility of thine own salvation - for none shall blame another for his own failure to heed - to come - for the Call hast gone forth -- I have sent Mine Servants far afield - I have sent Mine Emissaries - Mine Prophets - and now the Great and Mighty Host I have sent forth - that each and every one be touched - quickened - and awakened -- So be it I stand ready to give unto them as I have received of Mine Father -- I say unto them: Prepare thyself to receive of Me - as I have received of Him -- So be it and Selah --

Recorded by Sister Thedra

= Have They Heard Me? =

Sori Sori -- Let this Mine Word go forth - that they be spared the fate of destruction -- I say: Let it go forth - for them which will receive it - let them receive it and be as ones prepared to be delivered out --

The time is now come when they shall choose which way they go, they shall find the way of the wanton hard - they shall find they have betrayed themself - they shall find they shall wait another time - when they have prepared themself -- They shall be as the sad ones - crying for mercy - - they shall be as ones closed out -- Yet it is <u>now</u> said: "This is the day of atonement - the day of salvation" - - Have they heard Me? I ask: Have they heard Me?

= They are Confused =

I see them yet making merry - drinking and paying homage unto the one which enslaves them - they serve him - the one which holds them in bondage -- I say: They <u>are</u> <u>enslaved</u> - they think themself <u>Wise</u> - while he the enemy holds them in bondage - they fear him - yet they pay homage unto him -- So be it they are want to serve Me - and they fear the Light - - they know not which way to turn - for they are confused - they are a confused people - a lost generation -- I see them as bewildered - running to and fro - crying: Whither? Whither - and What - Why? Yet have they known not the cause of their confusion --

It is the way of the dragon to confuse - to divide and scatter - to bewilder and malign -- It is the way of the dragon to charm them by his deceit and flattery - and then turn his hand against them - for he offers unto them no solace in the end -- He laughs their plight - he gives no comfort - and he puts upon their neck - and they are bound by him - - and no remorse for his own part -- So be it I say: He is Mine enemy - and he shall be put to flight - for I am come to deliver out Mine - Mine Flock which shall turn unto Me for Light -- So be it I Am Come that they be delivered - - So let it Be --

I Am Sananda

Sori Sori -- This shall be Mine Word unto thee at this hour: The time is come when ye shall be as the hand made manifest - of yet another one of the Host -- He shall give unto thee a part which shall be for them which are fortuned to accept these Mine Words -- This One shall be Known unto thee for his wisdom - and his Light shall be unto thee great comfort - for he shall bless thee - and ye shall record his words unto thee - for he shall be as One of the Host - which shall come unto thee - and for this does he now speak - that others be prepared to receive of him -- This is his first speaking - - so be it profitable unto thee to accept him in the Name of the Father which hast Sent Us forth -- So be it and Selah --

Be ye as one on whose head I place Mine hand - and I bless thee with Mine presence -- I give unto thee this Word - and it shall be Mine blessing unto all which receive it -- The Word which shall bless them - the Word which the Father would have Me speak at this time - is for the good of all men - all peoples of all the world --

Yet they which are of the dark - shall know not that there is a Father - neither that there is a Host -- They shall be without hope - without Light - - yet I say unto thee: There is hope - there is Light - and the Father IS - ETERNALLY forever The ONE - The ALL - The Source of our Being - and unto Him All Power All Glory - All Praise -- So let it be - as He Wills --

We shall give unto Him All the Praise and the Glory - for the Praise is His - the Glory is His - and for this We say: "Praise ye Him"--

Mine hand I now extend unto thee - that ye might be as one prepared to receive Me - and it shall profit thee to receive of Me - for I bring unto thee a part which is for thyself alone -- While I give unto thee a part separate from thine - for them which shall receive that which is recorded for them --

They shall first receive the Word/ accept the Word - and then I shall touch them - and they shall know Mine touch and rejoice - for I shall bless them - and they shall know they have been blest -- So be it and Selah --

This I would say unto them which receive the Word: I come as One bound only by Mine Love for thee - for I have gone the way of flesh - I know the sorrow of flesh - the weakness of flesh - - therefore I come that I might add Mine Light - Mine Strength - Mine blessing - at this the dark hour of thy initiation - when the Earth is passing thru the trials and the pangs of birth --

I come that there be Light - that the Earth and the children thereof - be lightened of their burden - that their burden be lightened -- So be it that the Host comes that the burden of Earth be lifted -- It is given unto Me to speak for the first time thru one of flesh and I find it the way in which I shall be given the opportunity to do Mine part --

At the present I find no other thru whom I can speak - for there is none other which hast the power - the part to receive Me -- This is as new unto Me - and it is the way in which I shall do Mine service for a time - until I find one with whom I am able to make contact-- This contact - this one which hast received Me - is the hand of the Lord God made manifest - and for this am I able to use this hand so freely proffered Me --

So be it she shall be blest to receive Me and of Me -- I shall speak further on the subject of communication for a time - that there be greater understanding - and greater light on the subject -- So be it that I shall come unto others in the days ahead - as I find it expedient - and I shall add mine part - Mine blessing - Mine Light - Mine Strength unto theirs - for it is now come when great shall be the need of the Light - and it shall not be withheld from those prepared to receive --

Behold ye the Light -- Behold ye the Hand of God - See it move - and resist not the movement -- Give unto the Hand of God credit for the movement - - let it move -- move with it - for it is the Power of God which shall sustain and protect thee in thy trials - and temptations --

Pray ye mightily for Light - and it shall not be hidden from thee -- So be it that I speak from out the Silence - - the Silence is broken - and I shall speak again and again -- for this have I broken the Silence -- Amen and Selah --

* * *

Q. Is it permissible to record this - that I've just been shown?

A. Let it go on record - within the records - for them --

= **Revelation:** =

In the outer chamber; - My ward - "a young child" - and I - were in a room - where there was a bed - on which we rested - -

I saw upon a bookshelf - a great python - only his head showing between the books - -

I went into another room - where a father and his Carpenter Son were at work -- I told them that I saw the monsterous serpent on the bookshelf - and we dare not rest - -

The Carpenter Son came in - placed his strong - firm hand about the serpent's neck - dragged him down from the hiding place - -

As his great muscular body dropt to the floor - there spilled from his body - hundreds of small pythons - piles of them - -

I thot: O my - we are worse off than before! The Carpenter went back to his workshop in the next room -

I took my ward into another room - for its rest -- I sat watch - and then I felt a movement under my foot -- one had found its way into this room - - I knew we had yet to move into an upper room - - watchfully - carefully - -

Q. Shall I add anything - or let them interpret?

A. Add - The following lesson:

= The Vision =

Sori Sori -- Mine Word I have shown unto thee -- Ye have seen and known that which ye have seen - for it is revealed unto thee that which it is - - and it behooves Me to say: Ye have rightly interpreted what ye have seen --

Yet ye have not recorded the fullness of the revelation - for no written word can put it into words - - yet ye Know that which hast been shown thee --

= Interpretation =

The enemy lies in wait - - the enemy multiplies - - the multiplying goes on - and the multiplication is everywhere - save within Mine part of The Father's House -- Wherein is it said: "There are no enemies within Mine House"?

The enemy infiltrates into each and every part of thy house - the Earth -- Now ye shall be as one brot out - and ye shall be as one watchful and alert - for there shall be the offspring - infiltrating - penetrating into every crevice - - and they shall maneuver under cover and they shall be too numerous to count -- Yet these which are the offspring of the "parent enemy"- shall be as the young ones - not yet full grown - not yet full of strength and power - - and they shall be overcome before they are full grown - or of full strength --

These young enemies - by nature of their parent - shall be overcome easily -- yet they number in numbers untold - unnumbered are they -- They shall not mature to full strength - for I say: We of the Mighty Host shall find them - and deal with them in their youth - and they shall be removed in time - and put in the place prepared for them --

It is said - that the parent lies in wait -- he hast brot forth his kind - yet he hast been removed - into a far corner - and shall no more bring forth his young to torment and destroy a people - - a whole people hast he - the parent swallowed up -- Now it is come when many hast gone forth to do battle against his offspring - brot forth to do his work according to his will/ his nature -- Yet he shall not serve his purpose - for the Great Host shall do that which is give unto them to do - and he, the enemy - shall be defeated - ere there is another dawn --

Draw ye nigh unto Me - and I shall be thy Shield and thy Buckler, thy protection - thy strength - and ye shall Know no defeat - no harm shall come nigh unto thee --

Keep thy watch! Hold ye fast! Be ye alert - and be ye as one blest - for this I have said unto thee: "Come - follow Me - and I shall lead thee I shall give unto thee as ye are prepared to receive"-- So be it and Selah.

= **The Sweet Sonnet** =

Beloved: It is with great joy that I come - it is with great joy! - for I have sung mine sweet sonnet - and thou hast heard me - and responded. For this we shall commune this hour - - and let this go down thru the ages - as being of great moment - for it is given unto us to be as the forerunners of great events - Greater than thou hast Known or imaged for it is a new thing that we shall do - and a new thing shall be accomplished --

= **The Great Project** =

For this do we come unto thee -- And it shall be given unto us to be the forerunners of even greater events - - and on this occasion - I shall say: that it is our part to bring together the ones which are to participate in this our activities - in this the Great Project - and they shall be as ones prepared for greater - yet GREATER things - - for this is a New Project, yet long hast it been planned for this time - - it is said: everything is timed according to events -- So be it a truth --

Now it is come then we shall bear witness of that which is done within the Secret Places - wherein sit the Ones in High places - and we shall bear witness of their plans - their going and coming - and we shall participate in the activities which are fortuned unto us - that the way be made clear unto them -- There are ones which shall betray their trust - and they shall be as ones which shall be held responsible for their own folly - for they shall find that they have been the fool - and betrayed themself - that they have thrown overboard their own lifebelt - and they shall cry: "Help"- while they are sinking --

= Revelation with Wisdom =

While I say: It is the time of revelation - not all things can be revealed at this time - for not all could endure the things which shall be revealed unto them which are prepared -- The ones which are prepared shall receive in the measure they are prepared to receive - - none shall be given more than they can bear --

= The Testimony =

They shall have that which is necessary and expedient for the work at hand -- So be it I bring One unto thee which shall give unto thee a portion - and he shall be as one responsible for that portion - - then ye shall be responsible for that which ye do with it -- It shall be placed within the Book - and it shall stand as a testimony unto them which follow thee--

Now ye shall receive this One - and he shall come even as I - that ye be blest -- So be it ye shall Know him as the Brother from the land of the Sky - wherein there are places of Great Grandeur - wherein dwells Great Ones - far beyond thy ken - where walketh the Saints - which have come into the world of Light - and wherein they are born of the Spirit -- I take no poetic license - I am want to find words to describe that which I see - and know - in words which ye would understand - - for there are NO words available unto the human tongue which could describe that which I would that I could convey unto thee I say unto thee: Come - See - and Know - - be ye as one prepared -- So be it I bring this One with the consent of Our Teacher - the Counselor of Counselors - and the Mighty Host stands with Him in this his hour - for it is his first communion with the ones of Earth - since his departure. This is like unto his debut - and it shall profit all concerned -- So be it. Amen --

Sori Sori -- Let Mine blessing be added unto Mine Brothers' - for he hast brot me that I might add mine light - mine blessing - that I might share his joy - - and we find it the joy long awaited - for it is now given unto us to know the joy of contact one with the other -- And it is mine first experience such as this - and the first communication which hast been consummated by me - since first I came into this realm - -

= Communication =

This realm of Light wherein I find many which know the business of communication -- Strange it is to many - yet so natural to others - - fear is a great barrier and obstacle - and for this do they close us out - for we dare not impose ourself upon them which are not responsive unto us --

Now - it is said that we shall establish a line of communication - which shall <u>not</u> be broken - - therefore we shall progress - become more efficient - and of greater service unto the Whole - unto the Great Plan - While the Plan slowly and gently unfolds before us we shall move forward in perfect precision - in the Perfect Will of Our Father Which hast brot forth the Plan --

= Strange & New Work =

Therefore we shall do a Work which is New and Strange - unheard of by man -- Yet it is written - and truly so - that the Father's Will shall be done - and no man shall stay His Hand - - It shall move with precision and with surety - and nothing shall stay it -- Be ye as one prepared to go forth - and declare the Power and the Glory - unto them which are prepared to See - to Know - for nothing shall be withheld from them - when they are prepared to receive --

All mystery shall be removed - when they are prepared to See and to Know - - so let it be as they are prepared -- This is Mine contribution - - be ye blest to receive Me - and I shall speak again -- So be it and Selah --

= The Blessings =

Sori Sori -- By Mine own hand shall ye be led - and by Mine own hand shall ye be blest - Ye shall be as one blest by the Host - and ye shall be one of the Host - for have I not said: "Thy passport is in order"? Have I not said: Ye shall come unto me as one prepared -- So be it and Selah.

Ye shall stand with Me upon Mine High Holy Mount - and ye shall Know as I Know -- Ye shall do that which I do - go where I go - and be blest as I have been blest -- So be it and Selah --

= Devotion - Dedication =

Mine time shall be thy time - - thine time shall be Mine - and We shall do that which the Father hast Willed that we do -- We shall be His Will made manifest - and none shall be unto Us a barrier - for We shall go forth as a Mighty Army - as One Man - powerful and strong - <u>with Him</u>

as Our Power - for He is the Power - He is the Light - and unto Him All Power and the Glory --

= The False Ones =

It is said: Others shall come - declaring themself to be "He" - yet they shall fail in their efforts - they shall be brot low - for they shall not mock God and prosper - - they shall not mock God - and enter into the place wherein HE abides - so be it the Law -- They shall not partake of the joy of the Water of Life - for they shall be as ones cast ou

Be ye mindful of them which set themself up - and give unto themself credit for such power as they claim - and ye shall be as one which Knows the true from the false - and it shall profit thee --

= Silence =

While it is said: Ye shall remain silent for the time - - the time shall come - when ye shall speak out against them - ye shall stay their hand. Yet it is said: They shall - have no power over thee - and ye shall be as one blest to keep thy own counsel --

Ye Know the false One for that which he is - and ye shall have no part with him - - yet ye shall know him for that which he is - and give unto him no footing/ no quarter - for he is cunning - and he knows his heirs - he knows his agents and his partners - his disciples - - he rewards them with sweet promises and flattering words - - and they are the foolish ones which follow him - believing him to be their Messiah! I say: Poor in Spirit art they --

= Vain Promises =

Promises are promises - and they perish with the dew - - these are but his traps - <u>his</u> traps I say - for he - the one which they have given credit for being their Messiah - hast set a trap for them - and they are as his bait for others which follow --

Now they shall be, as ones responsible for their own folly -- It is said: They shall be promised "happiness" and glory in the Earth - power and ease - - while I say unto thee: These are his baits - in his traps - - put not thy foot into them --

Let him rave - let him boast of his power - - and give unto The Father the credit for thy Being - let the Glory and the Praise be His -- Fret not for the braggards - for they shall be brot low - and they shall not prosper - for I see them as finished -- So be it and Selah --

Place thine hand in Mine - and I shall lead thee gently and firmly - I shall give unto thee that which shall unto thee sufficient Light and Strength - I shall bring unto thee that which is needful - and ye shall not want -- it that I Know thy needs - and I am the One which Know and which hast provided for thee -- Be ye blest - and for them which seek the Light - that they be not ensnared - So be it and Selah --

* * *

I AM READING A BOOK BY ONE WHO CLAIMS GREAT POWER - - TO BE THE AVATAR OF THIS DAY --

IT TROUBLES ME - FOR THIS AUTHOR TALKS WITH A DOUBLE TONGUE --

I AM AWARE THAT MANY YOUNG ONES SHALL BE ENSNARED BY HIS WORDS - - -

THEREFORE I ASK: WHAT CAN I DO ON THEIR BEHALF? T.

* * *

= His (The False One) Method is Not New =

Sori Sori -- Beloved: Be ye as one blest to receive Me and of Me - and I shall give unto thee a part which shall be of great assistance - for there is much to be done - and ye shall be as one prepared -- let it be- and for this do I come -- While it is of great concern unto thee - that which ye have read - concerning the "new revelation" - it is not new -- The method is old - it is that which is pointed out - that which is foretold - the way of the dragon --

= Responsibility =

Now ye shall be as one alert - and fear not - for "the way of the dragon" shall hold no charm for thee - and ye shall be as one on whose shoulders fall great responsibility - for it is now expedient to give unto thee Greater responsibility - for Greater shall be thy revelation and they power -- It is said: - with Greater revelation and greater power - goes greater responsibility - so be it --

Let thine feet be firmly planted - and ye shall not slip - neither shall ye fail -- So be it that I am come to give unto thee assistance -- So be it and Selah --

= Part of the Plan =

Sori Sori -- Wherein is it said - that I shall touch thee and ye shall know thou hast been touched? Thou hast felt Mine touch and responded unto Me -- So be it I give unto thee this Word - - ye shall record it for them which have not responded -- They shall become responsive - for none shall be forgotten - none shall be overlooked - for it is the Will of Our Father that We go out unto them which are in flesh - as man of flesh - and touch them - that they might become responsive unto the Will of The Father which hast bidden us go forth --

= Concerning Generations Yet Unborn =

This is but part of the Plan -- The Plan as it is revealed unto us - includes the generations yet unborn - for as they are born thru the womb of woman - it is given unto them to forget their heritage - therefore we shall go with them - accompany them - and be unto them Guardians - Counselors - and Mentors - and they shall be reminded of their heritage their part - for which they came -- Let it profit them to remember --

Now ye shall be as one blest to be reminded - and in turn ye shall remind others - for it is said: "Ye shall go out amongst them as one free and ye shall touch them - even as ye have been touched - and they shall respond unto thee"- so let it be for the good of all -- So be it and Selah.

= Free Spirit =

Be ye as one free - and ye shall come and go freely - and y shall know that which ye do - ye shall remember that which ye do - and Know that which ye accomplish - - for it is now come when ye shall come into the place wherein I am - as on prepared - and ye shall return unto them - and give unto them an account of that which ye, have seen and found -

Let it profit them to learn of thee - and they shall be as ones prepared to receive of thee - - ye shall give wisely and prudently and none shall say unto thee:- ye are a fraud - for I say unto thee: Ye shall Know - and Know that ye Know! for I shall show thee - I shall teach thee - and ye shall Know that ye Know -- So be it and Selah -- Let it be as the Father hast Willed it -- Amen and Selah --

THEIR PROFIT

Sori Sori -- Be ye as the hand of Me made manifest - and. record the Word I say unto thee - - it shall profit thee to record that which I say unto thee - - it shall profit them which receive it unto themself -- So be it and Selah --

For this do I speak - that All be blest - - yet some shall mock Me - and some shall spit upon Mine Word - and these shall be reminded of their foolishness - in the time when they cry: "Lord - Lord" - for they shall remember that which they have done in the time of their wanton when they for the most part - was prone to think themself wise --

= Acceptance of the Servants =

These which accept Mine Word - shall likewise accept Mine Spokesman - Mine Emissary - Mine Handmaiden - - and Mine people shall Know Mine Servants - they shall honor them - and be as one of them -- They shall pay homage unto the ones which serve Me - which minister unto them without thot of reward - with selfless service -- They shall remember them -- and they shall be blest to remember them - for they shall be honored as they are prone to remember Mine Servants -- So be it and Selah --

I speak that they be reminded -- Wherein is it said: that "Mine Servants are Mine hands and Mine feet made manifest" -- So be it and Selah --

Forget not - Mine hands and Mine feet are Mine servants - - Mine servants serve Me - and I serve thee thru Mine servants -- So be it I give unto thee that which no man can take from thee - nor pilfer from thee -

when ye have made it thy own -- So let it be the Word I give unto thee this day - and ye shall be blest to receive it -- So be it and Selah --

= The Double Portion =

Bear in mind that I am come that All be blest - yet unto them which receive Me - I shall give unto them in double portion - I shall multiply their blessings - and they shall be glad -- So be it and Selah --

* * *

Sori Sori -- Be ye as one blest - and receive this Word unto thyself - and ye shall be blest - - I come that ye be blest --

Let it be known that there is an Mighty Host - for there are many which now move within the place wherein ye are - which are come - even as I - and they are come that there be Light -- So be it and Selah.

By the time they receive this - there shall be many which shall be quickened and brot out -- Many shall enter into the place wherein they shall go - unprepared (knowing not) - - many shall go into their places prepared (knowingly) - and these shall be the ones which shall be the ones which have heard Mine Voice and answered Me -- This shall be the part for which they have prepared themself - - they shall be glad for their preparation -- So be it and Selah --

Let it be said - that they which are prepared shall enter into the place wherein I am - without the poor part - which is the lesser part -- The lesser is fortuned unto them which hast not given unto Me credit for Knowing that which I am about -- So be it that I shall be sufficient unto them which heed that which I say unto them - and which come unto Me as a little child - for these I shall lead gently and wisely - and they shall be as ones prepared to go where I go -- So be it and Selah--

Fortune thyself to be one prepared to go where I go - for I shall give unto thee as ye are prepared to receive -- Amen - So be it and Selah --

* * *

Sori Sori -- Behold ye the signs of the New Day -- Behold ye the signs of the old day which fades away -- Be ye as on alert unto the signs of the times - and know ye that there are none which have prepared themself - that shall be without assistance - - and it behooves Me to say: I am come that ye have assistance in thine work - in thine part - within thine own place - and it is so -- So be it and Selah --

= "Death" and "Birth" =

Sori Sori -- Be ye blest this day - and give unto them this Mine Word - and they which receive it unto themself shall be blest -- So be it and Selah --

There shall be great uprisings - great upheavals - - yet I say - there shall be great rejoicing - for there shall be going and coning - - some shall go out - some shall come in - and there shall be greater Light upon the Earth -- For the ones which come nigh unto the Earth as the Host - shall bring Great Light and understanding - for they shall go by them - leaving a breath upon them - as a lingering fragrance - and they shall remember it - and they shall be as ones which have been touched -- They shall come to know the touch - and respond unto it - they shall be blest to respond -- So be it and Selah --

Wherein is it said - that they shall awaken in due season? I say it is now the time for many to awaken - arise and come forth as ones responsible for their part - - they shall be given greater responsibility and greater Light -- This I would say unto them: Many shall hear the Voice - Many shall see Visions - Many shall dream dreams - yet they shall be as ones prepared to Know that which they hear and see - and interpret the dreams they dream --

While these are the tools which We use to awaken them - We shall too - use even greater - more profound tools - which they know not at this time - for We bring even greater means of awakening the sleepers -- We shall prepare a part for them which shall revive - enliven them - and they shall arise as ones refreshed anew - and they shall be as ones awake - alert - alive - - and glad shall they be -- So be it and Selah --

= Serious Business =

Sori Sori -- Hear ye Me in this - and prepare thyself for the next part which I shall give unto thee - for ye shall now begin another book - which shall be different from the others -- This one shall be for them which hast gone all the way with thee -- It shall <u>not</u> be given unto them which hast turned aside - for they shall not be as ones prepared --

Now ye shall set aside the hours of the day which shall be reserved for Me - and there shall be NO interference - no disturbance -- The hours shall be at thy convenience - yet they shall be exact - and at the same time each day -- Then ye shall make known the time - and ye shall be as the one which sets the time - and none shall be unto thee a stumbling block -- Ye shall announce unto them thy intentions - and thy motives - there shall be no interference - for it shall be made clear unto them - that thy part is different from any other -- So be it that I am come that ye be prepared for the Greater part -- So be it and Selah --

= The Command =

Sori Sori -- Be ye as the hand of Me made manifest - and write this Mine Word - that it might go into the record - for them which follow after thee - them - which are prepared to go all the way with Me --

Now ye shall put aside all thy puny work for the greater part - for this is Mine time with thee -- Ye shall do that which I give unto thee to do - and ye shall fear nought - for I say: Ye shall do a Mighty Work which is fashioned for thee - - for this have ye waited - for this have I waited --

= Silence =

Now - it is come that ye shall stand as one with Me - and eye shall be as one prepared to do that which is given unto thee to do - - it is for this that I say: retire unto thyself - and set aside the time - the hour for our coming - wherein we might speak as One - for I say: The Mighty Host stands ready to assist in this - the Great Surge - against the darkness -- So be it and Selah --

= One Qualified =

Ye shall receive this one which I bring at this time - and ye shall be unto him Anchor - for he hast not spoken unto thee - - for that matter he hast not spoken unto one - since he hast come into his new place of abode -- Now ye shall go before him as a lamp bearer - that he might learn that it is for the good of all - that he speak unto one -- Yet the "one" shall multiply and grow into great numbers - for he is now qualified to speak - - for this is he permitted to enter into thine place of abode - - for this are ye permitted to receive him - for I am watchful - I am thy Doorkeeper - and for this do I see and know the qualifications of each one which is permitted to enter herein --

Be ye blest to receive him and of him - for he is now come - even as I am come - that All be blest -- Hear ye him and be ye as one blest to receive him --

* * *

Be ye as the one to receive Me – for none other hast received Me - none other have I spoken to/ with - for they are deaf unto Mine Voice - - Mine touch hast not quickened them -- The Plan hast unfolded unto Me/ us here - that we shall do a part within the Plan - and for this we are prepared -- I stand as one prepared to go where I am sent - and to do that which I am given to do --

This is the part which is given unto Me <u>now</u> - this hour - and the way shall be opened for greater work -- Greater Light shall be given unto us - greater responsibility - greater power - for by the ones which stand with Me as One - and together - am I given greater power - greater strength --

= **The Weapon of the "Host"** =

Ye shall be as One with Us - and the union shall be consummated - not to be broken - for in union there is strength - in strength there is power. So be it that the way is now made clear - for Us of the "Host" shall go forth as One Mighty Army - and We shall set strait the <u>crooked</u> - the crooked shall be made strait - and there shall be great rejoicing - for a great battle shall be won - and it shall be without the weapons of man -

it shall be with the weapon of Light - Light shall be our only weapon - for it shall be the weapon given unto us of The Father Which hast given unto us the Plan --

= Love of Righteousness =

The Plan - designed and executed by/ within the Light - is that which brings into focus the Love - the Wisdom in which - with which - we are concerned -- Let it be the Love of Light - the Love of Righteousness which motivates thy every response unto the Word - for none shall pilfer or destroy the Word - none shall tear down the House of the Lord by their own selfish motives -- I say unto thee: Close ye thy door - let them which would usurp thy time - find another door thru which they might enter -- So be it and Selah --

They which would rob thee of thine time - are but thieves and robbers -- I say: Close thy door - and shut them out -- So be it that I am come that I might bear witness of thee - and give unto thee of Mine strength - - likewise I am come that I might be as One better prepared to reach them which are given unto Me - - for by thine own Light and obedience do I learn the way in which to proceed unto Mine own -- For it is long that I have been from them - and they have remembered Me in word only -- They perpetuate Mine name with great arrogance and pride - yet they deny Me as being alive and responsible - as one who could reach them - as a "Spirit" -- They would shrink from the idea - and cry: "NO! NO!! Not so!"-- So let them learn - let them know that I am alive - that I am not "the ghost of <u>Hamlet</u>"- that I am he - upon whose foundation they have built their fortune - their great wealth -- Their pride they take from the name which I made - which they inherited from Me as their forerunner --

I say: They have builded unto the winds - they have accomplished nought - save their own downfall - for fall they shall -- Is it not said: "Pride goes before a fall"? It is so - - While they are about their boasting, their merrymaking - and their mockery - I shall be as one prepared to give unto them a part - which they shall at first reject - yet I shall hold it up before them - and I shall remind them of it until at last they shall hear - see - and heed that which I bring unto them --

I shall reveal unto them a plan - and give unto them details of the plan - so far as it concerns them - and they shall be as ones alerted - and they shall act upon the plan - as revealed unto them -- So be it that it shall concern thee and thy Work - - for this does it become necessary that certain things be accomplished - before the plan can be executed - Therefore I say unto thee: Be ye as one prepared to do that which is given unto thee to do - so be it that it shall profit thee -- Now ye shall stand ready to receive Me and of Me - for I shall call thee at another hour - and we shall speak further on this subject -- So be it and Selah.

= Their Sins Shall Find Them Out =

Sori Sori -- We shall continue our communication - for it is with communication that we are concerned now - at this time -- The ones which have builded upon mine foundation - upon mine name - shall fall and they shall be as ones exposed for their fraudulent sayings - and their pillage -- They shall stand shorn of their self-glory - and then they shall cry out for mercy - for they shall be exposed - - They shall stand naked.-

Wherein is it said: "There is no hiding place"? There is no hiding place -- I see them which are wont to cover themself with mine name - as fraudulent - as traitors - for I builded mine foundation on honor - and integrity - on the just law - of Service -- While I see them placing their yoke upon the neck of the workmen - the servants - making them subservient unto the plan which is designed to hold them slaves --

I shall stand before them as the accuser - as the one which hast come to bear testimony of their evil doing -- They shall cry for assistance - and their cry shall be heard - and they shall do that which shall justify the assistance - then it shall be given - with wisdom and in love --

Now it is said: that they shall cry out for assistance - then when they have made proper restitution - they shall be assisted in the way in which they should go -- I have learned - that they shall do that for which they came to do - that which they came to do - was to be unto their bretheren assistants - stewards of a great wealth - which was to assist the ones which were in need - the ones which had <u>earned</u> the assistance - so properly provided by and thru the foundation --

This foundation of which I speak - was given over to them which are now within the world of men - as provided by law - and they have not provided for them which were the ones which have earned their assistance -- They have gone far afield - that they glorify their name - and do honor unto themself -- They are prone to seek of man recognition - that they might be glorified -- So be it I say: They shall be brot low - they shall cry out for the assistance of the Host - and they shall come to know the meaning of "Assistance" – They shall be as ones prepared to accept our assistance - therefore they shall make restitution - and come with clean hands - and bring themself as ones prepared to receive their assistance --

It is said: "Ye shall have no false gods before thee" - yet I see them bowing before their false gods - their altars of great charm - and of great price - - yet wherein do they profit thereby? They have sold their birthrite for a poor penny - they have betrayed their trust --

I say: They have betrayed their trust - and it behoove me to raise my voice against them - for I am the predecessor which built up the foundation on which they have amassed their fortune -- So be it they shall be as ones responsible for their folly - for they shall stand in judgement as ones adjudged and condemned - for they have been like unto the traitor - they have bound themself by the law of justice - to be adjudged - they have perjured themself --

So be it they shall find themself unprepared - they shall find they have closed the door on their own fingers -- So let it profit them to learn of me - for I shall bear witness of their wickedness - their transgressions -- So be it and Selah.

= Sananda =

Sori Sori -- Upon thy head I place Mine hand - and I bless thee and give unto thee the blessing which shall be thy blessing - for I say: Ye shall be especially blest by Me and of Me -- So be it and Selah --

While it is come that others speak - even as I - I shall be thy Gate Keeper - the Porter at the Gate - and none shall enter in without sanction for they shall not pass unnoticed - unseen - unprepared -- They shall be as ones qualified and sanctioned by the Council -- So be it I bring this One which has spoken at an earlier hour - - ye shall now receive him - and he shall give unto thee another part which shall be added unto the other - - so let it be for the good of all -- Amen - and Selah --

= More Light - New Understanding =

Sori Sori-- Be ye as one prepared to receive me and I shall remember thee - for it is now come when we shall work as One - One mind - One purpose - and we shall bring great Light and understanding into the places wherein there is little Light - wherein they have not had the Light of the understanding which we bring --

It is said: - that they shall awaken -- By what means shall it be accomplished? It is said: - that a great Light shall come forth from out the East - and it is so -- So be it that the Light shall flood the Earth - and they shall see it - and some shall rush forward to greet it - while others shall shrink back in fear - and wonder at the manifestation thereof -- It is said: They which fear - shall be as the one which fail their Calling/ which are Called - but fail to answer - - for fear shall they turn their face from the Light and these shall be as the ones which have not heard that which hast been said – they have not been as ones alert they have not seen that which hast been shown them – they have failed in their haste to see – to learn – to know what is shown – what hast been said – That which hast been recorded for them hast not been unto them the lesson learned - they have not found the peace which comes with the understanding of the Word - either that which is spoken or written So be it they shall return unto the Word - and apply themself - and seek the Light - and it shall be revealed unto them --

Fear not them which know not - fear not them which would ridicule thee - fear not them which would flee from thee - fear not for them which would give unto thee the bitter cup -- Praise ye the Name of Solen Aum Solen - and be ye glad that this day is come -- Give unto Him all the Praise and the Glory -- Rejoice in Him and be glad -- So be it I shall speak again and again -- Let is be for the good of all --

= Now - This Day =

Sori Sori -- Let it be Known that the time is <u>now</u> come - when the Host hast gone forth - as the Ones which shall touch them - as the ones which shall awaken them -- This is the Plan thru which the masses shall be awakened, thru which they shall be alerted - - and they shall be quickened unto the touch -- They shall first be awakened - then they shall <u>Know</u> they HAVE been touched --

= Prayer =

Let every one be touched - let every one be quickened - let every one be glad for the quickening -- Let every one be filled with joy for his quickening - for he shall be as one come alive -- So be it and Selah --

* * *

Sori Sori -- Again let us speak of the foundation which is builded upon mine name - and they which have perpetuated the name which I have bequeathed unto them --

They which are the custodians of the <u>name</u> - and the wealth which hast been accrued - thru the foundation which is founded upon mine name - have been as weak of Spirit - they are poor in Spirit - they have lost the Spirit in which the foundation was formed/ laid -- They have been as ones taking credit unto themself - for <u>their</u> <u>Spirit</u> <u>their generosity</u> --

Wherein have they been as ones giving of themself - as a sacrifice the self-sacrifice -- They have lost sight of the Spirit in which I labored that others might be blest - and profit by my experience -- They have been as ones born of the wind - they have passed this way - and shall be known no more - for they have left not anything of themself that men remember them --

They stand stript of all their pride - self-glory - self-styled glory - for they shall face the tribunal which deals out justice -- I come that they which may read - might know that their conceit/ deceit – and power which is pilfered - shall avail them nought save misery and humiliation --

Humility is no part of these - mine heirs - for they know not humility - yet they shall see the humble stand in their places – glorified, arrayed in fine linen – and wearing the Breastplate of Righteousness -- So be it they shall see the humble sit with the righteous - and they shall find themself as ones unprepared - unfit to enter in -- So be it I speak that which is necessary - that which is expedient and profitable - for it shall go down in history - that I have spoken out in behalf of Justice and Truth --

Now ye shall enter into thy record - this my word – and it shall stand as a testimony - for them which shall read -- I put not mine finger upon them - yet unto them which have eyes to see - let them see - - them which have ears to hear - let them hear - and be ye not curious - for it is not of thy concern --

Let it be revealed unto them to whom it is of concern -- Be ye not concerned for that which is of no concern unto thee - - yet that which is of thy own concern shall be revealed unto thee So be it and Selah - - wait the next--

= Sananda Speaks =

Sori Sori -- Be ye as the hand of Me - and record this Mine Word - that they might Know that which I say unto thee - - be it such as shall profit them --

Be ye as one on whose head I place Mine hand in Holy Benediction and ye shall be blest of Me and by Me -- So be it and Selah --

By Mine own Word shall they be blest - and by the Word shall they be made Whole -- So be it - and Selah -- Give unto Me credit for Knowing that which I do - that which am to do - -and that which I do shall ye also do - for it is given unto Me to prepare the way before thee that ye might follow in Mine footsteps -- So be it I say: "Come follow ye Me"--

Thou hast heard Me - and followed where I have led thee - yet thou hast not finished thine Work and thou hast not as yet finished thy Mission -- So be it it shall be finished and ye shall be glad -- So be it and Selah --

Thine hour hast not come - when ye shall put aside thine pen and paper - for there is yet much to be done - much to be said - and accomplished - - so let it be for the good of all -- So be it and Selah -- Put thine hand in Mine - and I shall lead thee into Greater Heights, greater fields -- So be it - and Selah --

Put thine foot on Higher Ground - and stand with Me - and I shall show unto thee that which ye have not seen -- So be it ye shall rejoice with Me - and We shall rejoice together -- So be it and Selah --

= Communication =

Sori Sori -- Be ye as one blest to receive Me and of Me - for this do I come at this hour - - precious are the hours of our meeting -- So be it that I set aside the time - and I treasure the time which is allotted Us for such communication profit them which shall learn from such let it be communion – So let it be as The Father hast Willed it - and Selah --

By the Word do we communicate - and by the Word shall they learn and by the Word shall the Word be revealed unto them in its fullness- So be it and Selah --

= The Key - The Word =

First they shall seek Light - the Light from which cometh Truth and Wisdom - - from which all true revelation cometh - which is for their own profit and upliftment -- It is given to Us of the Host - to see them struggle with the "Mysteries" - looking for the "Key" - - yet the Key comes thru and by the Word - and the application of the law - for none is trusted with the "Key" without proper preparation - - and then it is revealed unto them - - for it is not found in print - for it is given unto each - direct and discretely - and unto them which have been found trust worthy -- None other need look for the Key unto the Inner Temple - for it is hidden up from the unjust and the imprudent --

The traitors shall be the traitors - yet they shall not find the Key whereby they may enter for I say: <u>None</u> pilfer Mine warehouse - none enter into Mine place of abode - none pass Me unaware - for I am not asleep - - I Am NOT amongst the dead - - I AM THE SON OF THE LIVING GOD - Sent that they might KNOW AS I KNOW -- So - let them come by the Gate and they shall be as ones prepared - even as I. So be it - and Selah -

= So-Called Christians =

Sori Sori -- This I would add unto the other part of the record - that is: Many of the ones which use Mine Name so freely - have not been disciples - - they make a mockery of that which they - do- and preach - so proudly they proclaim their service unto Me - while I see them as bigots - and they defame Mine teaching -- They are want to put their fingers in their ears - for they think themself the chosen -- While I say: They are want to be as the one chosen - they are not Mine disciples - they are not "The Chosen"-- By their fruit are they known - by their Light are they found - - and I see them as wanting --

Be ye was one which hast the Word -- Be ye as one prepared to follow where I lead thee - and ye shall be blest -- Bow not before the altar which they set up -- Be ye as the hand of Me made manifest - and be ye as one blest of Me and by Me -- Fret not for them which would misuse thee - and ye shall stand firm - and ye shall be mindful of the "Word" - and apply the law - and none shall set foot against thee --

Praise ye the Name of SOLEN AUM SOLEN - and ye shall be unto Me Mine disciple - for I shall forget thee not in the time of trial - in the time of thine afflictions -- Be ye as one mindful of them which serve thee - and ye shall not want -- So be it and Selah --

= They Shall Accept the Word =

Sori Sori -- This Word I would give unto thee for them which would follow where I lead them: - They shall follow Me willingly and freely, none shall be brot against their will -- So be it that I have called unto them - I have sent Mine Messengers unto them I have given of Mineself that they be brot out of bondage - and they have but to come of their own accord -- So be it - and Selah --

Now they shall <u>accept</u> the WORD - answer Mine Call - and follow in Mine footsteps - and I shall not fail them -- So be it that I Am "He" which is Sent that they be brot out of darkness --

They shall do their part - and I shall do Mine - and We shall go forward unto Greater heights -- So be it - and Selah --

= The Unseen Class =

Sori Sori -- This I would say unto thee at this hour: - Put aside thy puny work - and bring unto the altar that which hast been given unto thee - and be ye as one prepared to bless others which come unto the altar for a part with thee - a part which shall bless others which come to learn-

Ye shall be as teacher unto them - even as ye were unto thy Papa- and he shall be as one to bring them unto thee for this part -- and it gives us great joy to see them so eager to learn - - therefore I say unto thee: Be ye as one prepared to assist them - even as ye have assisted thy Papa - So be it and Selah --

While ye shall now rest - ye shall arise at the appointed time - and they shall gather for their lessons -- So let it profit thee to receive them even as ye receive Me -- So be it and Selah --

Recorded by Sister Thedra

= Sons of God by Adoption =

Sori Sori -- For this hour let us speak of fear -- Fear - is the barrier between the Host and the ones which have closed Us out -- Fear is the greatest barrier - - they have been hoodwinked - they fear ridicule - they fear the evil ones - they fear being misled - and deceived by the false one --

Yet - they have been given "The Word" and it says: "Fear not for I Am with thee" -- They have been as ones bound by the false one - - now they are as ones which know not that which binds them - they are want to be in darkness – they to let go that which they are accustomed to --

= The Paradox =

They know not that they are directed unto the Light <u>by</u> <u>the</u> <u>Host</u> - and they have been indebted unto the Host by their "Scriptures" - their Holy Writ - and their Sacred Writings -- They pay homage unto their unknown Benefactors - while they deny the existence of Them which stand by to assist them - NOW - THIS DAY --

They are not aware of THE HOST - which are at this present time amongst them - as their Assistants - their Benefactors --

It is said: They pray unto the unknown gods - while the 'Host" reaches out a hand to assist their ascent - their progress--

While it is unlawful that They give unto them their selfish requests or put their hand within the till of another - that their petitions be granted - is lawful that they directed in the way of the righteous - for the Good of All--

There are ones which are directed - while others do not take direction - they spurn the efforts of their Benefactors to guide them --

They are like unto a branch which hast been bent - and broken*- - they shall be pruned and shaped - and cultivated - and then they shall be as part of the Whole - in which they shall fit --

There shall be a great cry go out for the assistance of the Host - and they shall go forward in Great numbers -- They shall do a mighty work and they shall know that which they are to do - and do it they shall - according unto the law --

They shall be as the hand and foot of The Father made manifest - for They shall touch the unknowing ones - and they shall awaken and alert themself - and then they shall Know they have been touched -- THEN - they shall be as ones directed - they shall know from whence their direction cometh --

They shall follow the direction for it shall be their salvation - - and for this do We, "The Host" go forth that they might Know - that they might become the "Sons of God" by adoption -- So be it and Selah --

By adoption - I say - for they which sleepeth are but the sleepers - until they awaken - - then they shall arise as ones awake and alert - and come forth as ones prepared for their part - and which shall be given unto them by rights of adoption and they shall be as heir of The Father which hast Sent Us unto them -- So let it suffice that We are come that they awaken -- So be it and Selah –

* (I had been looking out over the snow-covered landscape - where many trees are broken - which will have to be attended to in spring. T)

= The Atomic Bomb Test in Nevada* =

Sori Sori -- There be few which are prepared to accept the Word of God as it goes forth - yet it comes swiftly - when many shall accept - and these shall be found and prepared for the Greater part - - for this hast the Host been Sent forth - as the Hands of The Father made flesh --

Think ye that the Host is not prepared for Greater things - Greater Work? Greater yet shall They do - for it is given unto Me to know the fullness of Mine Work -- Yet I cannot say what the fullness is - neither do I Know the fullness of The Plan Mine Father hast yet for Me --

The fullness of the Plan which concerns thee - the children of the Earth - and the Earth - I do Know - for it hast been shown Me -- And this I Know well - for I am One of the Council - - I am One of the Supreme Council - and it is given unto Me to Know the Plan which pertains unto the Earth and its inhabitants -- So be it and Selah --

Fret not over other worlds - other plans for them – fret not for the other planets - while thine own is in want - peril! PERIL - I say! For She stands in need - She cries out for assistance - for help - and I say: Help cometh swiftly and surely - and none shall say Me nay! for I Am He which is Sent that She - the Mighty Star - be delivered out of Her bondage --

I say unto thee: "BEHOLD THE HAND OF GOD MOVE - SEE I MOVE! - and be ye as one glad this day is come -- So be it and Selah-

By the time there is another dawn - many changes shall take place and none of the traitors shall be left within the Earth - within Her borders - for they shall be removed into another place - wherein they might learn that which they have not learned within the Earth --

The Earth hast given footing unto an ungrateful "Child" - and it shall be removed into a far corner - and it shall find that it hast betrayed itself and its trust -- It is said: "Honor thy own father and mother" -- The traitors hast not honored The Father - and they have disgraced their Mother - and brot disgrace upon themself --

Now they shall find they shall atone for their deeds - - they shall atone in full - and pay the last farthing for their folly - and transgression.

Transgressions are transgressions! the price is high - the atonement sure -- The time swiftly comes -- when the TRAITORS shall find themself in another place - another environment -- THEN - they shall cry: "Help" - and Our assistance shall be withheld until every farthing is paid -- Paid in full! I say - - Paid in full! --

Let them learn the price - let them turn unto the Light - and follow the Light - and they shall profit thereby -- So be it I have raised Mine Voice against them - - I have spoken softly - I have whispered - - and I have given them sweet sonnets - - I have been unto them all the Father would have Me be - yet they go headlong into the pit -- I now Cry - "Come follow ye Me" - yet they hear Me not - heed Me not --

= Judgment =

Therefore I raise Mine hand against them! I shall smite them - - I shall put before them barriers impenetrable - and they shall not enter into the place of Mine abode - for they are as ones unprepared - and they are as ones drunken on new wine - gone mad! - they are as ones gone insane they are as ones drunken on new wine!! - they are sick!! - and there is a place for the sick - the insane/ mad -- So be it - I Know - for this do I say: "A place is prepared for them"- it is So --

I say: They shall be placed in the compound - wherein they shall be given assistance - and they shall be as ones prepared for another place, another time - another part -- This is the Word I would give unto thee at this time -- So be it that I have spoken - and thou hast heard Me -- So be it - and Selah --

*(Sent a blast 8000 ft in the air)
 (A news item)

= So Often We Forget =

Sori Sori -- For this hour let us share the joy of our communion - of our coming - and the joy of being received - and the joy of receiving - - so be it such that others shall come to know -- So be it that I go forth with great joy - great anticipation - knowing that there is a great number which are with Me - that they might come to know that they are not alone --

It is said: Man walks not alone - - it is so - for he is not alone - he is NOT alone! nor is he hidden from our sight -- We know where he is, where to find him for there is no hiding place --

= True Knowledge =

There is a part which hast been withheld for this time - and it is now come when man shall come to know what is meant by the "Host" - when they shall walk and talk with us as One - when they shall differentiate between the Light and the dark--

It is said: "There are ones which would lead thee astray (evil ones) Ride thy back (possess thee) - yet these have not come as ones prepared to lift thee up - - they have come to do mischief - to enslave thee" - - it is now come when they shall know the one from the other -- They have been told that which shall prepare them - they shall know them by their "fruit" -- They which come bearing witness of the Light - ask no favors set no traps - and give of themself that others be blest - - they give of themself in selfless service - asking no reward --

= Braggards =

While the ones of darkness come in their own name - bearing witness of themself - <u>their</u> "<u>good</u> <u>deeds</u>" - and they strut themself before man - and boast of their greatness -- I say: Behold him - in his conceit - - know him for that which he is --

See the one who stands watch - he which stands in silence - asking nought but to serve in the Name of the Most High --

These are the Servants of the Most High -- THESE are the "Avatars" - the ones which have made the supreme sacrifice of SELF - they serve selflessly - and with joy --

= By Their Fruit... =

Know ye them by their fruits - - it is said that a tree which brings forth no fruit - is better than the one which brings forth bitter and poisonous fruit - for it shall be up-rooted and cast into the fire - for it is no longer profitable for the poison to be about - - and it shall profit them to know one from the other --

Take ye note of the BRAGGARD - for he is as the braggard - he is mighty in his own eyes - and powerful in his own words - for he hast a good opinion of himself - he THINKS himself wise indeed --

= The Fool =

Yet he maketh a fool of himself - for he is known for that which he is - he is seen as a fool - and a fool knows not that he is foolish - he <u>thinks</u> himself wise - therefore he is wont to see his foolishness - he is wont to know his foolishness - he sees himself as great - - and proud is he of his own portent - of his own part - which he hast portioned out for himself - - for he is not aware of the Great fortune which awaits him - when he is prepared to receive it --

Let it be said: He shall be brot face to face with his foolishness - - his folly shall be unto him a mockery - and he shall turn away from it in shame -- So be it he shall learn the way of the Servant of the Most High Living God - - so be it profitable unto him - - for this do we stand by - that he might come to know there is a plan - by which he may be brot out of his bondage - and be forever free -- So be it and Selah --

So be it as The Father would have it --

= Unity / Strength =

Sori Sori -- Be ye as one on whose head I place Mine hand - and I shall bless thee thrice - and again I shall bless thee - for I am come that ye be blest always - and forever - - So let it be --

This word I would give unto thee: There are ones which have come with Me - and each and every one leaves with thee their blessing - their love and appreciation for thy assistance in <u>their</u> work - for it is a union of strength - even as "the bundle of sticks" - - and where there is union of effort - there is strength -- While one alone is not of great strength - when there is union and oneness of purpose there is GREAT strength - So be it that we are One in this Mighty Army - which is sent forth to do battle - and to give battle against the forces of darkness -- So be it that We know what We are to do - and the method by which We are to accomplish it --

This I would say unto thee - - let it be for the good of all that I say it unto thee:-- There is a <u>Plan</u> - and in this Plan are many which have been prepared to do the Work - which is to dispel the darkness of the past - the superstition and ignorance - - this is the part of the Host - of which I am but One -- I now speak as <u>One</u> - of Mine own volition - from my own experience - from my own heart I speak -Yet there is but One Mind here within the place wherein we abide -- Think ye not that we have no place - no headquarters - no place of operation! for is it not said: "As above - so below"?

It is so - - The Father's Plan is far superior unto man's plans - yea - they are small indeed - for the plans of men are small indeed - compared to the Great and Divine Plan - brot forth and executed thru the Mighty Council -- Wherein is it said - that the Council hast sent Us - the Host forth to execute this part of the Plan of which I speak --

This day we are as ones prepared for <u>this</u> Our Part - - and there comes a day when Our Part be finished - and we shall be given other parts - and each shall be within the Great and Divine Plan -- We are but the executors of the Plan - which deals with <u>this</u> phase of the Work - the WORK of God The Father - - for by and thru the hands of His Servants does He work His Wonderous Work --

His Will be done in us - thru us - and by us - and for us -- So let it be -- Amen and Selah -- Will it not be a glad day - when we shall see the Whole of the Plan - when the Sons of God shall sing together as One?- Amen and Amen - So be it - - Selah -- Sori Sori -- "Let the light shine in - let the light shine in"* - - This shall be my sweet sonnet this hour - for I say unto thee: The Light shall shine forth as never before - -

There shall be great Light which shall be seen by many - and there shall be some which shall go into the next realm - knowing not that this day is come - the day for which they have waited -- <u>They</u> shall be as the sleepers - and <u>they</u> shall sleep on - while the Light shall be the Light unseen by them which sleepeth -- So be it that they shall have their awakening in another "School" - wherein they shall learn well their lessons - wherein they shall find themself --

This is the Word I would give unto thee at this hour -- So be it and Selah --

*These lines are from an old hymn --

= Promptness & Responsibility =

Sori Sori -- This is My time with thee - and ye shall be as One with Me and we shall give unto them this Word -- as it shall profit them to receive it -- So let them have it as it is given unto thee - - so be it that they shall be blest to receive it -- So be it- and Selah --

This is the appointed hour for this Our communion - and it is My joy to come at this time - for there is much to be done - and great shall be the results of Our Work --

While ye may not know the fullness thereof - I say - thy part is important unto the Whole - - thy part is necessary - therefore it is said: Ye shall be as one responsible for thy part - for it is said: "Ye shall be as one responsible - and with greater responsibility goes Greater revelation"- it is so -- So be it that there are ones which <u>ask</u> for revelation - which are not <u>as yet</u> responsible for such - - they are not as yet prepared to receive that responsibility - which goes with greater revelation -- So be it that We of the Host have prepared Ourself for Our part - and accept the responsibility that it carries with it ---

There are ones which ask for responsibility - which are <u>as yet</u> not prepared to accept it -- These are as the children which ask for adult machinery which would destroy them - for they but set into motion the <u>Word</u> which they shall reckon with - for as they ask - so do they receive not always that which they ask - - yet the power of the Word is a mighty weapon in the hand of the unlearned - as well as the learned -- So be it that they ask - and are not prepared to take the responsibility of the manifestation --

There are ones which ask - knowing nothing of the responsibility which goes with the manifestation - - they too are unlearned in the powers accompanying the Spoken Word -- There are ones which ask in silence - - these too create and bring forth that which they ofttimes reject - and deny as their creation - - they refuse to father their child which they have brot forth -- So be it and Selah -- It is So!

There are ones which give - asking nought -- These are as ones which have given no thot to the results of their giving - - these shall find that they have created without thot - that which shall be brot to light in many ways - - some shall be as the "tack in the shoe"- some shall bear fruit bitter unto the tongue - - others shall be as the rose which blooms upon the thistle - which is truly abominable -- It is the way of the unlearned to give without thot - without considering the results thereof -- Consider well the motive - - consider well the asking - and above all - the wisdom of thy giving -- So be it that there is <u>wisdom</u> in giving - WHEN given wisely --

There are ones which give for the asking -- These consider not the wisdom of their giving - - to what purpose? to what purpose do I give unto this one? for what purpose hast he asked of me? To him I would say: Consider well the use which shall be made of thy gift -- Ask not of him which asks - rather consider the fruits of his labor -- Hast he tilled his fields - hast he planted to his profit? Hast he planted thorns and thistles? Hast he planted the grain and herb to his profit? These things I would have ye consider - and it shall profit thee --

Now let us consider the man which hast tilled his field - brot forth the harvest which hast blest his labor - and the rains came - washed away his harvest -- then he is without the substance to provide for himself -- Then consider well his plight - and be ye as one considerate of his plight -- provide for him a plenty - that he build back his loss - and become again self-responsible - and thy assistance shall be profitable unto all - for it is the law --

Consider well that which I have said - and it shall profit thee -- So be it and Selah --

I Am the Porter -

= Sananda's Blessing =

Sori Sori -- Come ye forth and be as one on whose head I place Mine hand - and I shall bless thee with Mine Presence - and with My being - for I shall remember thee - and give of Mineself that ye be blest --

Let Mine hand be thine - and I shall be unto thee great strength - and ye shall do a Mighty Work - and ye shall be as one with Me - for I shall be unto thee all The Father would have Me be -- So be it and Selah.

= Obedience =

Thou hast heeded that which I have said unto thee- - now ye shall be as one blest to know that which ye have not known - and ye shall profit thereby -- So be it and Selah -- For this day - let Us be about The Father's Business as One - and for this have I called thee out from amongst them - - for this have I brot thee hence - - for this do I attend thee -- for this have I placed upon thy head Mine hand in Holy Benediction -- So be it and Selah --

I have given unto thee in Great measure - that ye be prepared -- Thou hast given unto THEM that which I have given unto thee for THEM - and thou hast not betrayed thyself -- So be it that ye shall be given in Greater Measure - and it shall profit thee -- So be it and Selah.-

Be ye as one prepared to receive that which is prepared for thee - and ye shall give it unto them which are prepared to receive it -- So be it that they shall receive according to their capacity -- So be it the law.- Amen and Selah --

Arise at the appointed hour - and I shall bring One unto thee - and ye shall receive Him as One of the Host - and ye shall be blest to receive Him - and of Him -- So be it and Selah --

* * *

Sori Sori -- This would I say unto thee this day - and ye shall give it unto them which are of a mind to receive - for it shall profit them to receive it unto themself - for it is according unto the law --

There shall come unto thee ones which have been as ones seeking the Light in the places of darkness - for they are under the yoke -- they are as ones which have looked unto people - things - and places for their light -- they have not found it - for they seek within the realm of man - and they find not that which is the Light - - for it is by their own effort that they increase their light - and by <u>their</u> Light are they found-

They shall first seek the Light which is the CAUSE of their BEING, then they shall be diligent in their search - and they shall be given every consideration - and they shall be given the necessary assistance - and guidance -- So be it and Selah -- For this do I say: Prepare thyself to receive of Me - - this is Mine Word unto them which are want to be delivered out -- So be it and Selah.

* * *

Sori Sori -- Be ye as one prepared - for this day I say unto thee: There are ones which have within their hand the power to smite thee - and it behooves thee to be prepared to meet them face to face - and it shall profit thee to be as one prepared -- So be it and Selah --

While it is said: They have within their hand the power to smite thee - - I say: Stand ye steadfast - walk ye tall - and ye shall not fall - for I am with thee -- So be it and Selah --

= The Will to Follow... =

Sori Sori -- I now give unto thee a part for them which have the will to follow Me - and ye have but to record that which I say - and it shall profit them to receive it -- So be it that they which receive it unto themself shall be blest -- So be it and Selah --

I am He which hast sibored thee - and I have sibored thee well - for thou hast applied thyself - and been as one true unto thy Calling -- So be it that I shall give unto thee of Mine Treasure House - of Mine part that ye be prepared for Greater things -- Yet there is much to be done - so let it profit thee to finish this part which hast been given unto thee to do - then - ye shall find that ye have accomplished great things - while knowing not the part ye have played in the Great and Divine Plan --

= The Test =

To them which have the will to follow Me - I would say: Harken ye unto that which I say unto thee -- be ye as one tried - tested as by fire! and be ye as one trustworthy - and willing to follow where I lead thee for I shall lead thee into fields afar - and in ways strange and new unto thee - that ye be prepared for the Greater part - that ye be prepared to go where I go - - and ye shall prove thy worth - and ye shall be as the Servant of the Most High living God - and ye shall Know the joy of Service -- Ye shall do that which I do - and ye shall Know as I Know - So be it and Selah --

Bless thyself by thine own effort - and walk ye in the way in which ye shall go - and be ye as one blest - - so be it I shall do Mine part -- So let it be as The Father hast Willed it -- Amen and Selah --

***

Sori Sori -- Swift is the thot - swift the flight of thot - and swift are thy hands to obey the thot sent forth - for thou hast obeyed - and now ye shall be as one blest - for ye shall be as one responsive unto the thot sent forth - and ye shall Know that ye have received the thot - - so let it profit Us - and for the Good of All - let it be -- Amen and Selah --

= Upon the Firm Foundation =

Sori Sori -- Upon this Rock I have built Mine House -- Upon this Rock I have set up Mine Altar - whereupon I have placed thee - as Head of the House which I have founded - upon the Rock --

This is Mine House - and I have builded it upon a firm Foundation and it shall stand -- So be it and Selah --

I have brot unto thee these Mine children - upon whose head I shall place Mine hand - and I shall bless them as I have blest thee - and I shall give unto them that which shall profit them -- So be it and Selah.-

While I am about it - I shall bless them as none other - for I shall do a wondrous Work thru them - and I shall favor them - for they shall do that which I give unto them to do - - and I shall give unto them a part which shall be for the good of All mankind -- So be it and Selah -- For this night let it be said that there is One amongst thee that would bless thee as none other - - for this hast he come into thy midst --

He hast within his hand the power to bless thee as I bless thee - for he is One with Me - and he hast his hand upon the tiny one - which is his ward - and he shall be as her parent-guardian - and she shall Know him for a time - - yet she shall forget in time - for it is the way of flesh to forget yet she shall be caused to remember him in days ahead -- So be it and Selah --

For this hour - let it be said that I am with thee - and ye shall be blest of Me and by Me -- So be it and Selah--

= Christ's Word =

Sori Sori -- For this hour let us rejoice that this hour hast come -- Let us rejoice together and be glad -- So be it that We of the Host draweth nigh - not for a day - <u>not</u> for a night - but for always - - for We shall not turn aside for time nor event - for the event hast come - "The Coming" consummated - and We come in Great Glory - which they see only faintly as thru a glass darkly --

They which sleepeth - sleepeth - yet the Word hast gone forth: "I AM COME" - and they know it not - for they have not been touched. They shall be touched - - and it behooves them to respond unto the touch - and come forth as ones prepared to receive the "King of Kings"

They are wont to speak of the King - yet when He sends forth His Messengers to tell them HE IS COME - they turn a deaf ear - they are prone to persecute them - and be as the oppressor unto them which I send forth as Mine Messengers -- So be it that I AM COME - even as promised - yet they have misrepresented Mine Word - and "The Coming" - - they have not seen nor heard that which was meant by The Coming in GREAT GLORY - - yet hast the Word not been fulfilled - This Day!

So be it that I Am the Host of the Host - the Host is the "Host" and One with Me - - They come even as I come - in GREAT GLORY --

Radiant are They - and born of the Spirit are They -- One with me are They - as of <u>One</u> <u>Body</u> -- And in the Name of Our Father Solen Aum Solen - do We go forth as One Body - made perfect in Him -- So be it and Selah --

= The Christ Message =

Sori Sori -- Let this be the Message I bring at this Season -- Let it be for them which seek the Light -- Let it be for them which ask for Light Let it be for them which have a mind to follow where I lead them -- So be it and Selah --

This is the Word which I would give unto them at this time - this Season: - This is the time of sobering - the time of meditation - the time of reflection - the time of looking forward -- Yet I see them looking backward - looking unto the "manger" - the empty manger - no longer holding the Babe - - I say no longer does it hold the Babe --

The "Manger" no longer a Symbol of the time - the Season - the birth of the One now Crying: "Come unto Me in Holy Surrender - Come as a little Child"--

The Babe is now no more - for the Age of Light reveals the One Sent - as the hour Grows Nigh for the Whole World to see - to Know that He is Come in Truth and Reality - that HE IS NOW COME - that ALL MEN might be lifted up --

While it is said: "I Am Come" - they seek for the sign - they look afar - they wait - - they know not that I Am Come this day -- I Am He Whom they await - yet they accept Me not - - they have been as ones looking in the closet for the Light - - wherein is there light in the dark corner?

They have thot to make of Me a thing -- In their imaging they have imaged a vain thing - for they have not seen the Light - the Light which I AM -- They have been as ones blinded by their illusions - their opinions - preconceived ideas of The Coming -- Let the Babe be no more - let the Living God - come forth within the World of Men -- Let the Light be seen - and known among men --

Let them walk in the Light Which I Am -- Let them bring forth fruit of their labor - acceptable unto the Father -- Let them Come - bringing themself in Holy Surrender - unto His Will Which I Am -- So be it I Am Come that they Awaken unto the Will of Mine Father which hast Sent Me -- So be it and Selah.- So let it be well with thee --

Recorded by Sister Thedra

= Signs & Miracles? =

Sori Sori-- Be ye as the hand of me made manifest unto them which would follow Me -- So be it I speak unto them which are of a mind to follow where I lead them --

This is the day of "The Coming" - the day so long foretold - and now they are as ones which are want to see - and know - - they ask for signs and miracles? - - have I not given unto them signs - which are written in the HEAVENS!? Have they read aright the written Word? Have they thot themself wise? Have they not seen the written Word? Do they believe that which I say?

Now it is said: I have sent forth Mine Messengers to herald Mine Coming - and it is said: "I Am Come"- yet they wait!

They prattle of "The Coming" - and know not that I AM COME - not as a new born babe - - it is not as a babe that I Am Come - - I am Come as the Word of the Living God made manifest - as the Son of the Living God made flesh -- I am Come even as I went - and I shall go again - even as then - for there be ones which know not I am Come - there are ones which Know Me Not! - and for them - there shall be another time - place - another day - another place provided for them wherein they might come to know --

There are ones which have full knowledge of Me - and Mine Mission - and these are as Mine Family - Mine Servants - Mine Emissaries - and Mine Brethren - the "Host" which are sent to awaken them which slumbereth -- So be it this is the day of awakening - - let it be as the Father hast Willed--

While there are ones which shall sleep on - it is of no concern unto thee - the time of their awakening - - I say: it is of no concern unto thee for they shall have their day -- The length of their sleep shall be of no concern unto thee - for I shall be unto them all The Father would have Me be - it is Mine concern --

I say unto thee: Be ye alert - and about thine own affairs -- List' ye unto Me - and bear ye witness of Me - and walk ye in the way I point - Let not thy foot slip - and ye shall apply the law unto thyself - and prepare thyself for the Greater part -- So be it and Selah -- I AM HE - which is sent that ye be brot out of darkness --

Now ye shall accept the WORD - or reject it - as ye will - - yet it is said: "Blest is he which accepts it - Blest is he which prepares himself to go where I go -- So be it and Selah" --

* * *

Sori Sori -- Hail Hail unto the Victor -- Hail unto the Victor - for he hast overcome - he hast overcome!! Hail! I say - for he hast overcome!!

Let it Be - - so shall it Be --

Now ye shall stand as One with Me - and ye shall sing the Praise of SOLEN AUM SOLEN forever -- So be it and Selah--

Let thine VOICE be heard - and let thy Works be known -- Let thy Light be seen from afar - and let them come - and partake of thy Praise and We shall Sing as Sons of God together - for it shall declare unto them that THE LORD IS COME -- So be it and Selah --

= Witness =

Sori Sori -- Long have I waited this day - this hour - when I might come unto thee bearing witness of the Host of The Living God. Long have I waited - long indeed -- While the time hast not lain heavy upon Me - it hast been the time of great preparation - when We of the Host have been preparing for this time - the time of the awakening - the time of going forth - that each and every man might be enlightened - and that none be forgotten --

There are ones which know not of Our existence - the existence of the Host - neither the Host of the Host - which bears witness of Us of the Host --

These are as ones which have been the fortune* of ages past - wherein they forfeited their gifts - misused them - or denied them -- They did not accept that which was proffered them in ages past - they betrayed themself --

*(Product - return)

Now they are again come into flesh for the purpose of learning - and giving of themself unto the Light which cometh in the darkness - - while the darkness comprehendeth not the Light -- We of the Host shall go forth as One Man - as One Voice - as One Mind - One Mighty Hand as One Great Surge of Power and Light -

And great shall be that Power! that Hand - and nothing shall stay it for it is the Will of The Most High Living God - that this day bring forth the harvest*-- So be it and Selah --

*(Resurrection)

This is the day long foretold - - and for this do We go forth that the way be made strait - that they be prepared for the Greater part -- So be it that We Know each and every place - every one - by their number - their color - their sound - their light*-- So be it and Selah --

*(The 5 string lute)

This is the Word I would give unto them which have a will to learn and to be delivered out of bondage:

There is but One Father - Which is called "God" - The Cause of thy BEing - the Source of thy Being - - and He is the Creator Supreme - - He hast created eternally - and it is GOOD - - He creates Perfectly!

None other creates Eternally - Perfect - for He is The Perfect - All Wise Living God -- Born of Him art thou o man - born of Him art thou! Eternal art thou - - not of a moment - not of a score - neither a century but Eternal!

The Spirit which thou art is not born of woman - for a span of time to decay and return no more --

While I bear witness of The Father and His Word - I say unto thee: Greater hast man been - greater shall he be - than he hast imaged - - for "Man" hast been as the Spirit - free from flesh - free from bondage - free from darkness --

Yet he chose to enter into the dense world of flesh - as flesh - and to walk as "man-of-Earth"- - and thru the womb of flesh came he as the animal - bound by the law of flesh - even as the animal is bound -- Now it is given unto him to be both man and animal - - the animal is but the flesh - - "Man" as created by The Father - perfect - is the Spirit Eternal for The Father created of Himself - thru the Spoken Word - and it was perfect in every respect save none --

The part which man hast chosen shall be unto him his Book of Life which he hast written upon the Pages of Time - which shall bear testimony of his travels - his travails - and his wanderings - and wonderings upon the periphery of time and Space - flung afar upon the horizon of the Universes of eternal space - - and the timeless parapets whereupon there is written his records - without error - with the precision of the gods which are appointed the keeping of the records --

I say: Behold ye the vastness of the Father's Domain which He hast created for Man - the Man of His Creation - that which He created from

Himself - from out His own Being - - this He Called Good - - it wast Good -- Therefore it is to be given unto this Eternal Being - to be brot back - even as it went forth - Perfect in every respect -- Therefore <u>The Host</u> shall go forth to awaken the "Man" which slumbers within the animal form --

For Man lies asleep within the form of flesh - flesh of Earth - and as such he is bound by flesh -- Therefore he shall come to know that he is eternal - and that he hast an inheritance - not of Earth - but of the Eternal Heavens - that which is his freedom from bondage –

The Inheritance kept for him from the beginning - - and for this do We of The Host bear witness of the Eternal Man - the "Spirit of Man - which is the part which is FREE! Free from the animal world -- We speak of "Freedom" - of "bondage" - and it shall be understood that bondage is of man's making - freedom is of The Father - offered unto thee at this time - when the sleepers sleep - knowing not that they sleep. They shall be as ones fully aware that they are in bondage - they shall seek the Light - they shall find - - <u>They</u> shall be freed -- So be it and Selah --

For this do We go forth as The Father hast Willed it -- So be it His Will that All be prepared to come forth - and accept their inheritance- So let it be -- Amen and Selah --

= To The Recorder =

Sori Sori -- By thy hand shall ye bear witness of Me - for ye shall record the Word for them - as I give it unto thee - and it shall profit them to receive it unto themself -- So be it and Selah -- Be ye as one prepared to give unto them this Mine Word - and it shall profit thee - for it is given unto thee to be as Mine hand made manifest unto them -- and they shall be as ones prepared to receive it- So be it and Selah --

This I would say unto them which have been unto Me Servants - and them which have heard Me and answered Me - they which have come forth that they might serve Me – selflessly.

= To Mine Servants =

Mine hand I shall place upon thy head in Holy Benediction - and I shall bless thee as thou hast not been blest - and ye shall Know that thou hast been blest -- So be it and Selah --

This I would have thee Know: It is given unto Me to be the Host of the Host - and I am the Porter at the Gate - - and it is for this that I say unto thee: "Pass ye in - for thou hast proven thyself trust worthy - and thou hast served Me fearlessly and selflessly - - thou hast asked nought but to serve the Light - for righteousness sake - for the good of all -- So be it - I say: thy reward shall be great indeed-- So be it and Selah" --

= Man's Journey =

Sori Sori -- By Mine own hand I shall lead thee - and ye shall be led aright -- So be it and Selah -- Fear not them which would be unto thee a "A poor priest"- them which would instruct thee in the way of the unknowing ones -- They speak of "The coming of the King of Kings"- "that He shall set up a Kingdom of God on Earth" - - yet it is said: "The Kingdom of God is within"- So be it! And too it is said: "None enter in save thru the <u>Gate</u> - the strait and narrow - <u>The Light</u> - - and it is for this that I Am Come - that they find the Kingdom within --

Yet the Story begins not with man - neither does it end with man- The journey of man is the way of man - back unto his place of going out - - his journey is but the twinkling of an eye in Eternity - - and yet he sees himself as but the beginning and the end -- The totality of man is not that which he sees or knows - - he is but the fragment of the Whole - - he is not whole of himself - he is but a fragment of the Whole!!

Man as such - is but the fragment of the Whole - the creation of The Eternal Solen Aum Solen - The "ALL" - The ONE --

This is but the beginning of man's sojourn in time - for his time endeth not with Earth -- He is a traveler thru "Time and Space" - thru Eternity - worlds without end - for he is Spirit - - Born of Spirit is he. There is but One Father Eternal - Solen Aum Solen - from which cometh All things - eternal - without end - without beginning --

Yet man as such - shall be the fragment - and as the Man made perfect - he shall return unto his Source as One with It - - and then he shall Know his Source - and he shall be One with It - and no more shall he see himself as fragments - for he shall be Whole - - Whole in word and deed - for he shall know which he is - and he shall no more go into darkness - as a wanderer upon the periphery of time-- So be it and Selah.

= The Servant's Reward =

Sori Sori -- This I would say unto thee: Let them which have the mind to follow Me - come forth and bear witness of Me and Mine Word - - let them stand up and be counted - - let them be as Mine hand - Mine foot - that Mine Work be done upon the Earth - as it is in Heaven -- So be it that Mine Servants serve Me whole-heartedly - without reservation.

They are as Mine hand and foot made manifest - - so be it that they ask nought save to serve with Me - as Mine hand and Mine foot -- So be it that their reward shall be greater than the Kingdoms of the Earth - for their reward shall not be of Earthly Substance - it shall be of Spirit - and Spirit is Spirit - - it passeth not with the substance of the Earth - as the substance of Earth -- So be it that the reward of MINE SERVANTS shall be as the Will of The Father - for He hast Willed that they receive their inheritance in full -- So be it and Selah --

They shall be as the Sons of God - returned unto their rightful estate So be it - and Selah --

* * *

Sori Sori -- By the hand of Me shall ye be led - - by the hand of Me shall ye be directed - and ye shall be directed aright -- No place shall ye fail - neither shall ye fall -- So be it that ye shall be as one prepared to enter into the Secret Place of The Most High -- So be it that I am with thee unto the end -- So be it and Selah --

= The Shining One =

Sori Sori-- It is now that I come unto thee in the Presence of the All-Wise - All-Knowing One - - Shining and Radiant in His Light - that out shines the Sun -- So be it I come that He be Glorified -- So be it and Selah --

Let it be known that I am come unto thee - for the purpose of giving unto thee this part - the part which shall bless thee - - it is given that All be blest -- While some shall reject it - ye shall accept it in the Name of The Father Solen Aum Solen -- So be it that I bring Mineself for His Honor and Glory --

I give of Mineself that He be Glorified - - and it behooves Me to say unto thee: No man comes unto Him - save by the Shining One Which out shines the Sun -- So be it He is the WAY and the LIGHT -- So be it and Selah --

Hear ye Me - and bear ye witness of Me and Mine Word - for I come in His Name - and by His hand have I been directed -- So be it and Selah -- Give unto Me credit for being that which I Am - and ye shall be blest of Me and by Me - for I come that ye be blest -- Hear ye this - and Know ye that I am not alone - for I come with a Mighty Host which are even as I - One with Him - The Shining One

The Host is The Host - The Mighty Army Sent forth that Man of Earth be brot out of bondage - out of darkness --

This is the Word I would give unto thee this day: Great shall be the awakening - for it is given unto Us of The Host - to go forward as a Mighty Onrush of Light - a Mighty Surge of Light - which shall banish the darkness - which shall be as nothing - for the Light shall banish the darkness - and it shall no more engulf a people which are now engulfed within it - - they which seek the Light shall come to Know that they are but part of the Whole - The Whole - from whence they sprang -- So be it they shall be remembered - and they shall be remembered - - they shall Know - and be Known -- So be it and Selah --

For this do We go forth - that they be awakened - alerted and brot forth -- So be it and Selah --

Fortune thyself to be one of the Host - and fear nought for there is nothing to fear - in this the hour of thy trial - when all seems dark about thee - for it is the darkest hour before the dawn -- While it is said - this IS THE DAWN - some have not yet awakened unto it - - the day comes swiftly when the Light shall shine forth as the MIDDAY SUN -- So be it and Selah --

= Listen =

Sori Sori -- Be ye as the hand of Me made manifest - and give unto them this Mine Word - and ye shall profit thereby - for it shall be for the Good of All -- So be it and Selah --

Bless thyself as ye would be blest - - so shall it profit thee to give unto them this Mine Word --

There is the written Word which is spoken - and written as it is spoken - - this is the part herein -- Now ye shall listen for the spoken Word - as it shall be spoken -- Hear ye that which is said - and ye shall be blest to hear - and to heed -- Yet the Word which is written shall be The WORD - and not to be discounted --

Ye shall first accept the written Word - and the Servant which brings it unto thee - - and ye shall then be touched and quickened - that ye hear - and Know -

Ye shall not image that ye have been touched -- Ye shall not put words into Mine mouth - for I shall spit them out -- Ye shall wait upon Me - and ye shall be Glad for thy waiting - for it shall profit thee --

Now ye shall not feign wisdom - - neither shall ye declare unto them thou hast been touched - for ye shall be as one silent and humble --

Walk ye in the way ye should go - - bear ye witness of Me - and ye shall do that which I give unto thee to do - - ye shall be as one blest -- So be it and Selah --

= Blessing =

Sori Sori -- Mine hand I place upon thy head - and I bless thee as none other -- So be it and Selah -- Hear ye that which I say unto thee - and be ye blest of Me and by Me - and ye shall be as One blest of The Father Solen Aum Solen --

= The False Ones =

Sori Sori -- Hear Me in this and be ye as one alert - for there are ones which come unto thee for the purpose of exposing thee - - and it is said: One shall come which shall be as the traitor - - he shall be as a traitor unto himself - for he shall bring with him his friends - and his enemies for he shall be as one which hast both friend and enemy -- So be it and Selah -- Wait - for the next word - and ye shall be given more Light -- So be it and Selah --

= Of Obedience =

Sori Sori -- This is Mine time with thee - and for this have I waited -- It is with great joy that I come - and it is with great joy that I am allowed to speak unto thee on the subject of obedience --

Let this be Our theme for this hour -- The word obedience is for the most part the poor part of discipline - and that which is to be the unwanted part - the unacceptable part of thy present society - the part which they so ardently reject --

Obedience is the Great part of preparation for Greater things -- It is the part which is so necessary in All thy preparation -- Obedience unto the Law - Obedience unto the direction of the Great and Mighty Council - The Counselor - the teacher - the parent - the director in thy Spiritual affairs and whither goest thou - depends upon thy direction - and thy direction depends upon thy obedience unto the Director - for He - thy Director - directs thee in the way ye shall go - - and thy part is to obey His direction --

Now it is said: Ye shall be as one alert - and ye shall be as one obedient unto thy direction - for it is come when ye shall be as one on whose shoulders rests great responsibility - and ye shall now begin a new part --

Ye shall set aside the time for thy communication - and be ye as one faithful in thy dedication - and ye shall have no other things before thy part - which is to accept that which shall be given unto thee to do - for it shall be of the GREATEST IMPORTANCE --

Let thine time be Mine time - and thy hand be Mine -- So be it and Selah -- Now ye shall begin thy new part on the morrow - and it shall profit thee -- So be it that ye shall set aside the time - and ye shall be as one prepared - and it shall be given unto Me to be the Door Keeper - and I shall be responsible for Mine part -- So be it and Selah --

Hear ye Me - and be ye as one responsible for thy part - - so let it profit them which shall receive of Me - and I shall bless thee with Mine Being and Mine Presence -- So be it and Selah --

= The Unseen Ones =

Sori Sori -- Be ye as one responsible for this Mine Word unto them which are prepared to receive it - for it is for them which are prepared to receive it - - none else shall accept it- - therefore it behooves thee to give unto the ones which ask for the WORD -- So be it that it shall profit them to receive it unto themself - - they shall be blest to receive it unto themself -- So be it and Selah --

The ones which have come - are but a few which are to come - - and they shall come in great numbers - and ye shall receive them in Mine Name - and they shall be as ones blest to come - - ye shall be blest to receive them -- So be it and Selah --

The ones which come shall be as the Host - and they shall be as ones prepared to give unto thee a part for them which have prepared themself for to receive - for the <u>Word</u> shall precede the manifestation - and it shall profit them to read - and receive the Word -- So be it and Selah -- They shall bear witness of the WORD and <u>then</u> - the manifestation -- The manifestation shall follow the Word -- So let it profit them to receive the Word - make it their own --

Yet I say: NONE shall pilfer the WORD - neither shall they make a mockery of the WORD -- It is said: "Woe unto them which make a mockery of 'The Word' " - for it is a mighty weapon in the hands of the unwary - the unlearned - - and it shall be the two edged Sword - it shall cut both ways -- So be it that I say: Be ye as one prepared to receive it in the Name of The Father which hast Sent Me -- So be it I come in His Name - - I Am His Will made manifest -- So be it and Selah --

= Purpose =

Sori Sori -- Let the time be - and ye shall be as one touched - and ye shall Know that ye have been touched - and ye shall come unto the Altar as one Knowing - as one prepared to receive -- So be it and Selah.-

Be ye as one prepared for this thy new part - and it shall go out unto the people as it is prepared for them - - and in no wise shall it be changed - for it is given unto thee for a purpose in this manner - and it is for this purpose that ye shall give it unto them in the fashion it is given unto thee -- So be it and Selah --

= Self Assurance =

Hold thy head high - walk ye tall - know ye that I have called thee forth that ye do Mine Work - that ye be One with Me in this - the Will of Mine Father - for He hast Willed that the Plan be brot forth in this day and ye shall see the Plan unfold before thy eyes - and ye shall be glad - So be it and Selah --

While it is given unto Me to see the Whole Plan - it is given unto thee to see in part - - yet thou hast not comprehended the fullness thereof --

Be ye as one alert - and bring thyself unto the Altar of The Most High Living God - that His Will be done - - let it be - - so shall it be -- Amen and Selah --

Be ye as one prepared to accept this One which shall bless thee with His Presence -- He shall give of himself that ye be blest -- So be it and Selah --

= The Christ Body =

This I would say unto thee: There are many which stand with Me - that they might bear witness of Me - that they might add their light unto Mine - that there be Greater Light - greater strength - - therefore We shall be as One in this - for We are of One Mind - one hand - one foot with One purpose - to serve the Light - the Life which We are -- So let it be unto His Glory - forever and forever - Amen --

= Giving & Receiving =

This is the blessing I bring - that I might add unto thy light Mine - that I might be strengthened by Mine giving and receiving - - this is cohesion of light force - it is the giving and receiving - the taking and giving - the change and exchange -- The precious gifts which are exchanged at this season - is but symbolic of the giving and receiving of each blessing which goes with the communication - - the thot - the touch - the quickening - such is this communication - a blessing -- The exchange and the coming together as One - as Brothers of the same Order - - and within that Order We shall be as One - as the Will of The Father Which hast given unto Us BEING -- Blest are We to be of the Order of Melchezedek -- So be it that We shall be as ones prepared to bring forth Greater Light and understanding - within the realms of man wherein he wanders - for the most part in darkness -- He hast not known the mystery of Life - from whence he came - his origin - neither whither he goeth -- So be it he shall be enlightened - and for this have We been sent forth into his realm at this time -- So be it and Selah -- For this hast thou received Me -- For this have I come -- So be it as The Father hast Willed it --

* * *

Sori Sori -- This is the Word I bring unto thee at this hour: The time is now come when the way is made clear - that the Host might come into the world of men - as the forerunner of the Great Day - when the Sons of God shall gather together to Sing the Praise of The Most High Living God - for the part which hast been accomplished within so short a time.

The day swiftly approaches - when the Sons of God shall sing together as One - with the Great Joy which is theirs alone: "Praise - Praise unto The Most High - for He reigns and All is Well"--

So shall it be - - so let it be - for all is Well - - All is Well - for He reigneth Supreme! So be it and Selah--

= Mine Servants =

Sori Sori -- There are the ones which hear Mine Voice and heed it - - and there are ones which hear it and heed it not -- And unto these I would say: Be ye as the ones which have not heeded - and ye shall wait for a time - - then ye shall know that ye have not given thyself unto Me as Mine Servant - for Mine Servants do that which I give unto them to do - and they are not found complaining - - they are as ones gladly giving and gladly receiving --

So be it that these which have not given unto thee of their substance - of their wealth - their store - that ye be succored - that ye be supplied - shall be cut off for a time --

Then they shall learn that to give is to assist Me in Mine Work - for the Word shall go forth with or without their assistance - yet the ones which assist shall be blest by their own effort - for by their own effort shall they bless themself -- Let them know that they shall be as Mine

Servants and they shall do their part - - their part shall be to assist and provide for thee the necessary help - for this part which I have given unto thee --

So be it that I am at the Head of This House - and I have said that Mine Servants shall maintain it in order - and I have set thee over Mine House called the--

GATE HOUSE

And they which are so blest to receive these words - sent forth - shall be as ones to provide for the maintainance thereof -- So be it that they shall profit thereby -- So be it I shall bless them as they have blest themself - for I shall add Mine Blessing unto theirs - and they shall be thrice blest -- So be it that I have placed upon thy head Mine hand in Holy benediction - and I have given unto thee this part - and it is for this that I have commanded thee that the Word go out unto them which are of a mind to serve Me - of the mind to receive of Me -- So be it - I have spoken - and thou hast heard Me - and obeyed Mine commandment -- So be ye blest of Me and by Me - for I am come that ye be blest --

I Am Sananda

Recorded by Sister Thedra

Sori Sori -- Let this day be the New Day - the day of change -- Let the change profit thee - and it shall be a glad day -- This is the day of joy and gladness -- So be it and Selah -- Now ye shall return at a later hour and I shall give unto thee a part -- So be it and Selah --

= Dedication =

Sori Sori -- Be ye as one prepared to give unto Me thy undivided attention - and it shall profit thee -- So be it We shall have Our communion at the hour indicated - and it shall be as thou hast planned. So be it and Selah --

By the hand of Me ye shall be led -- Fear not - for I am thy Director, thy Elder Brother - and I shall lead thee every step of the way -- So be it and Selah --

= Obedience =

Be ye as the hand of Me - and record that which I say unto thee - and it shall be given unto them which are prepared to receive it - for none other shall accept it unto themself -- This I would say unto them at this time: -

The ones which are prepared to follow Me shall be as ones favored for they shall go where I go - - they shall enter in - and We shall rejoice together -- So be it and Selah -- Be ye as the one which hast prepared to go where I go -- So be it that I come that ye might go where I go - and ye shall be glad forevermore --

I say: Ye shall be as one blest to go where I go - - So let it be -

I am come that ye be prepared -- So let it be As The Father hast Willed it -- Amen and Selah --

= The Loss Shall Be Turned to Gain =

Sori Sori -- Let this be Our time of communication - and it shall be for the - Good of All -- So be it and Selah --

By the time shall We be brot together for this communion - and it shall be as none other -- So be it that I am now come that ye be blest -- So be it and Selah --

= St. John: 17-9 =

There is but One Lord God - and there is but One Time - - that time shall be Mine time - and I shall not count the hours of the day - neither the year -- I shall not count the days nor the years as lost - for I shall count the profit thereof - knowing the profit to be the harvest thereof - I shall not tire of reaping the profit thereof --

While the loss shall be the loss - I say: The loss shall be turned to gain - - therefore I The Lord thy God - shall wait for the harvest - wherein I might cast in the sickle and reap unto Mine own self - that which is Mine - - and that which is not Mine I shall reject - I shall put aside - for I pilfer not that which is not Mine -- I accept no poor penny, I accept no counterfeit - neither do I accept a bribe --

I am Porter at the Gate - and I know Mine own - for I have placed upon them Mine Seal - - and Mine own Knows Me - and they are come of their own will -- So be it and Selah –

= The Cry: "Be ye as one Prepared!" =

Sori Sori -- Let this be Our time in sweet communion - for this We come - for this We are glad -- So be it We shall be as ones come in One accord - and it shall be for the Good of All -- So be it and Selah --

This time is allotted unto Me as spokesman for this Mine family - the Voice of one crying from afar: "Be ye as one prepared to enter in" "Be ye as one prepared to enter in" - "Be ye as one prepared to ENTER IN!"--

= Operation Awaken =

Yet they have not heard - they have not given ear unto Me -- They <u>shall hear</u> - for I shall call unto them until they have heard - - I am not to be turned aside --

= The Silent Servants =

There shall be others which shall do a Work unknown unto them which have turned a deaf ear unto Me - for each shall have a part in the awakening -- We shall call it: "Operation Awakening" - and it shall be as an operation - for they shall be as ones prepared for the operation - - they shall be touched - quickened - and their ears shall be made to hear their eyes shall be opened and they shall see - and know -- So be it that we shall be as one prepared to stand by - until each and every one hast awakened - and until they are brot forth as ones responsible for themselves. So be it and Selah --

Bring forth the blind - and bring forth the deaf - - let them be made to see and to hear - - for this are we now come forth - that they may see and hear and Know -- So let it be -- Amen and Selah -- Be ye as one glad this day is come - for it is said: "This is the day of awakening" - - it is so - so be it and Selah -- Let us rejoice that it is So --

Now ye shall rest - and we shall continue on the morrow--

= Each Unto His Own Part =

Sori Sori -- For this hour let us discus's the part each is given -- Thy part is to accept us for that which we are - and the Word which we give unto thee - - the part which is given unto "them" - that they might know that which goes on behind the <u>Door</u> - the part which they shall play after they have gone the way of <u>so</u> <u>called</u> "death" - - that they might be as ones prepared for their new part - when they enter into their NEW Place - - that they might not fear their "New Part"-- This is necessary - they know not <u>how</u> necessary - yet we say it <u>is</u> necessary --

= Faith First - <u>Then</u> Knowing =

This is their part - - Ours is to be as the forerunners of the Word - that they be prepared to accept the Greater part-- The Word precedes the manifestation - and the manifestation is the fortune of them which believeth on the Word -- So be it that the ones which accept the "Word" shall be blest by the manifestation of the WORD - the fulfillment of the Word - or - the WORD made manifest -- So be it and Selah --

This I would say unto thee: The Word is the fulfillment of the Law and unto them which receive it unto themself -- So let it be -- Amen and Selah --

Fear is the Great barrier - - fear is the biggest barrier -- Yet there are ones which know not that they fear - neither that which they fear --

= Fear of "Death"? =

They have no notion of the thing they fear -- While they imagine a dark foreboding - they are fearful - and it behooves Me to say unto thee: It is the thing they fear which haunts them - - the haunting fear shall be theirs - even after they enter into their new realm --

They shall learn that there is nothing to fear - there is nothing save their own fears - their own unknowing - their own part which they have carried with them -- For this hast it been said: "Put from thee thine own preconceived ideas of and about Me -(Sananda) "-- Put from thee thy own puny concept of thy new part - and come as one prepared to do that which is given unto thee to do -- So let it profit thee - so shall it be well with thee --

Let them which are of a mind to learn - learn from that which is said within these lessons - if lessons they be - for it is given unto Me to see them learn - - and likewise I see some rejecting that which is so lovingly given - that they be prepared for that which they shall find - when they pass the portal of <u>so</u> <u>called</u> "death"--

It is said: "There is no <u>death</u>" - it is so - - it is but an awakening -- While it shall be gentle - and with great care - it behooves them to be as ones fearless - lest they sleep longer - and their fears infest them more --

= Escapists =

There are ones which would forever sleep -- These shall have their time their day - - these shall come to their full time - and be as ones alerted.

= It's of No Concern to Thee =

There are ones which deny their eternal existence - - these too shall come to know -- While there are ones of darkness - which shall pass and be no more seen - these are of no moment - no concern of thine - nor Mine - - be ye not concerned for these - neither fear for them - neither ask after them - for these are NO CONCERN of thine!

Be ye about that which is given unto thee to do - and that hast been clearly defined unto thee -- So be it and Selah -- Rest and be refreshed and we shall continue later--

= Concerning the Records –Ishmail =

Sori Sori -- This be Ishmail - it is I - Ishmail speaking -- Let it be for the good of all that I speak unto thee at this time -- It is said: I am the Keeper of the Records - - certain Records are given into Mine keeping and I am responsible for them -- It is of great import that I say unto thee: Be ye as one responsible for the records in thy keeping - for they are of great concern unto Us - - yet none within thy midst know the value of such - for they are as yet young in the way of the <u>wise</u> - and they have as yet not seen the value of these records --

None shall find therein the value - until he hast passed the bar - "The Bar" - then he shall come to Know the value of such as thou hast so faithfully kept --

These records shall be as the <u>Records</u> in the days ahead - for it shall be as the Light in the dark -- It is said: "The darkness comprehends not the light"- it is true -- While the records shall be as the written testimony of the many - thy Benefactors - the Host - and the Host of the Host - they shall be kept as such - until such time that they serve their purpose.

These records are but duplicates of that which is faithfully kept and written in gold - upon the pages of time - within the <u>Book</u> <u>of</u> <u>Life</u> - not to be erased - - forever shall they endure - as The WORD of God - for by His own hand hast He caused these records to be kept - and they shall endure --

For this I say: Be ye as the custodian of such records as hast been given unto thee - for them which are to follow thee -- So let it profit them to read - see - and Know the value thereof - for it is clearly stated that they which are prepared shall receive - - and it is so - So be it and Selah --

* * *

Ishmail called several times before I answered -- Then he announced himself as the "Keeper of the Records" -- He is no stranger to me - for he has spoken before about these records -- Thedra -

= After "Death"/ The Awakening =

Sori Sori -- For this hour let us come unto this Altar - as ones prepared to receive that which is kept for us - - That which is kept is the Greater part - for our work but begins - when we enter into the place which hast been prepared for us - when we put aside the temple of flesh -- It is said: "It is but the beginning of thy learning"- the grade one - shall we say - - while there are many grades to pass thru while in flesh - the Spirit is not confined to the "First grade" - the lowest grade -- While the flesh is the temple of the Spirit - it is not the "prison" - it is the temple which Spirit hast <u>builded</u> - and it is built according to the law governing the flesh - that it might endure within the realm of flesh for a certain time - then it shall be as the dust which it is - and it shall be as the substance of the Earth - which it is!

= Of Spirit =

There is much to be said on that subject - yet we shall speak of the Spirit which is not as a prisoner entrapt within flesh -- When man learns that he is as a free being - he will have won his first part - for this is as his degree - shall I say --

He shall see himself as free - for he shall no longer see himself as one entrapt in flesh - for he shall know that he is free - and he uses his temple of flesh for that which is he hast chosen to do - - and then he shall be as one responsible for that which he does - for it shall be but the beginning of his learning -- That which he learns he shall remember and it shall profit him --

= Man has Read the Letters Only =

Man hast seen the words - read the letters which compose the words - he hast placed much stress upon certain words - certain letters - knowing not the Greater meaning - that which is the Spirit of the word They have put their own interpretation upon the Word - and lost the Spirit of it -- So be it I bring unto thee the simplicity of the Word - the purity of Spirit - and ye shall not embellish it in any manner whatsoever for it is the way in which it shall be given unto them which are prepared to receive it -- So be it the that I am come that it be simplified so let it be clear unto thee that I am sent for that purpose--

Despoil not the Word of Spirit by the embellishment of it - "for their sake" -- Let it suffice that it is given unto Me by the Great and Mighty Council I come -- So be it and Selah --

= The Door Keeper Speaks =

Sori Sori -- Be ye as one prepared this day - to receive One which comes from afar - for he shall come as One prepared to give unto thee a part which shall be for the Good of All -- So be it and Selah --

By the hand shall I lead thee and I shall direct thee - and ye shall fear nought -- So be it - I bring this One that ye might come to Know him - and that he might Know thee -- So be it that this communion shall profit thee -- So be it and Selah --

Sori Sori -- Be as one prepared for to enter into the Secret place wherein ye may partake of that which is prepared for thee - and ye shall be as one blest -- So be it I bring with Me this One which shall bless thee by his presence - and he shall give unto thee a part which shall be for the Good of All --

Now he speaks of his own accord - and that which he says is his own word - and of his own free will does he speak - for he hast come forth of his own account - of <u>his</u> <u>own</u> <u>free</u> <u>will</u> - - and I have set upon him Mine Seal - for he comes thru and by the consent of the Mighty Council -- He bears the Seal of the Council of Councils - for it is given unto Me to Know - and I say unto thee: His passport is in order -- So be it and Selah --

Be ye blest to receive Me - for I bring unto thee a blessing as none other - and ye shall come to know Me - - and for this shall we be as the Servants in the House of the Lord -- So be it and Selah --

This I would say unto thee: It is fortuned unto Me to have passed thru the Earth in times long past - and I have gone a Great way - - yet the way I have gone hast led unto Greater heights - Greater learning - understanding - and Greater Glory --

This is the way in which I have been directed - and I have followed in the way revealed unto Me long ago -- I have not wearied of Mine lot, Mine part - I have gone strait ahead - and borne Mine part with strength and joy - knowing that I am not alone -- Never was I alone - for I walked with the Shining One - and I took great comfort from the Presence of this Great and Mighty One which is the Beloved --

So be it that as I stand within His Presence - I bow - and give thanks to Our Eternal Father for His Goodness - His Grace - Mercy and Patience -- For His Goodness I do praise His Name - - for His Mercy I do give thanks - - for His Patience I do rejoice - and I shall sing His Eternal Praise forever -- So be it and Selah --

Hold ye steadfast - and bear ye witness of His Mercy - His Goodness - His Presence - and ye shall rejoice with Us - the Host --

= Gloom/ Restlessness / Impatience =

Let it be said that there is no gloom within the Realm wherein We are We see gloom as darkness - - and impatience as a tempest - the seas tossed about - - and the restlessness of men - we see as the rushing of the winds upon the storm tossed sea -- So be it the winds shall be stilled the waters shall be calmed - and there shall be Peace -- Let there be Peace within thee - - weary not of thy part - and fear nought -- Rest assured thou art not alone - for thou art One with the Host - and it shall be Our part to sustain thee - and to bless thee -- So let it be -- Amen and Selah -- -

* * *

Sori Sori -- While this is but the beginning of Our Work - We shall work together as One - with One mind - One purpose -- So be it that I come unto thee for the purpose of serving the Light - the Light which lights every man which cometh into the World-of-man -- So let it suffice that I am One of the Host - come by the consent of the Mighty Council -- So be it and Selah --

This I would say at this time: The way is open - the law is clearly defined - and the Host stands by -- While they "Stand by" - they are not as ones without action - they are not idle - - they are as Ones busy - alert - and about The Father's Business -- So be it and Selah --

The time is <u>now</u> come when the Ones of the Host shall pass among them which are yet in bondage - and they shall be as the ones which shall be guarded - guided - touched - and awakened - - the ones which receive the Ones of the Host - shall be brot out as the ones prepared -- they shall be liberated - and set free -- So be it that first they shall accept The WORD - then they shall accept the Host - for the Word precedes the Host -- They have been told - - have they accepted?

Now they which have accepted - and put their hand out - are the ones which shall receive in full measure --

These which cry for assistance shall receive in the measure they are prepared to receive - - yet they shall be as ones prepared to receive in Greater measure - before they find they have received the <u>Greater</u> <u>Part</u> The Greater Part is kept for them until they have grown unto their full stature - become mature -- THEN - they shall comprehend the meaning of freedom - Love - and responsibility -- they shall <u>then</u> be as ones accountable for themself and their part - - they shall <u>then</u> know that which is fortuned unto them to do - - they shall do it with grace and dignity - and with humility -- So be it and Selah --

This is Mine Word unto them which have a mind to receive it -- So be it and Selah --

= Help for an Uncertain World =

Sori Sori -- I come unto thee declaring the Truth and Light - - the Light I bring with Me is the Light Eternal - the Eternal Verities -- So be it I am One of the Host - - Come am I - even as the others have come - thru the Council of Councils -- I bring unto thee Love and Compassion for the world - the world a-totter - the world a-staggering - this world sick and afrighted --

The World of men - now no longer secure in their own realm - - the world of men - no longer secure of their own wisdom and judgment -- I say: With all their learning they have not become wise - for they have not learned the first lesson set forth - the lesson of Love - for they have made a mockery of the Word - they know not the meaning thereof.

Now it is come - when they shall put from them their hypocrisy - and be up and about The Father's Business -- They shall become aware of that which hast been said herein - they shall be as ones blest to be aware - and they shall be aware of their part - - they shall see themself as they are - not as they think themself to be --

First they shall seek the Light - -

Then they shall see with eyes of Spirit - and Know that which they have not known -- So be it that they shall be as new born - born of the Spirit - and all things shall become new -- So be it and Selah --

= The Door Keeper - The Various Doors =

Sori Sori -- Be ye as one called - and be ye as one which hast answered the Call - - and Know ye that it is well that ye have answered -- So be it that I say unto thee: There are none so deaf as those which hear not.

The time is come when ye shall receive from the One which comes from afar - and ye shall give it unto "them" as it is given unto thee -- So be it ye shall be blest to receive of him -- This is the part which he hast prepared for thee - - receive him in Mine Name -- so be it that he hast Mine Seal upon him --

= The Plan Unfolds =

Be ye as one <u>blest</u> to receive Me - for I come that All be blest -- Now ye shall come into the knowledge of the part which thou hast played in the Plan which now unfolds before thee -- So be it that I am the Porter ye shall know Me as such - yet I am not the Lord God Sananda - - I am One with Him - - while I am the Porter within another place - another part of the Created Universe of Universes --"Within The Father's House Are Many Mansions" - Mine is a far distant One -- and of Mine own realm I speak - - far beyond thine at present - for it is said: Ye are on the periphery - and it is So -- Mine place is not so far out as thine - and the / is yet greater - brighter than that which comes thru into thine realm for thine is the dense world - "The world of darkness" - the world of doubt - fear - and uncertainty - the world of men is the dense world --

The part which is given Me is the part which is portioned unto Me of the Same Father Solen Aum Solen - Which hast given unto The Lord God Sananda His Part - His Station - His Office if you will - for He is the Porter at the Gate thru which ye pass - into the Greater Realm - as ye go from "Glory unto Glory" - and as ye pass thru the various places, "Doors" - on thy return unto thy abiding place -- So be it that I reach out Mine hand and I touch His - - He reaches out His hand and touches thine - - now ye shall reach out thine and touch a multitude within thy own realm -- So be it that I have opened the Door into Mine Realm - and ye shall enter in - - and likewise ye shall return unto thine own -

that ye bear witness of Me - and the Kingdom in which I reign - in which I dwell --

I say unto thee: I am the One which hast come into the world of Man - even as thou art - for the purpose of adding Mine Light - Mine Love - Mine Energy - that there be More Light - and that Man might come into his heritage - that he might be as one lifted up --

The time is now come when he shall put aside All his preconceived ideas of his journey thru time / space/ and ∪ - - for this has the Door been opened up unto thee -- It is said: Ye shall pass thru - - enter ye is and be ye blest - - blest to enter - blest to return unto thine own -- While it is said: "Spirit is free" - it is truly said - for ye shall come in Spirit - and return in Spirit as ye come - - as ye come - so shall ye go -- So be it that ye shall be the fore - runner of Me - and ye shall be as Mine hand made manifest unto them which shall receive Me - - for I shall reach out Mine hand in Holy Benediction - and I shall bless them which would accept Me and Mine blessing --

Let them hear that which I say - and understand that which I say - for I say unto them: There are many Mansions within Mine Father's House - - Mine place is but One - over which I have been set - as the reigning King - the One which hast the same responsibility for Mine "House" as the Lord God Sananda hast within His House - and as such we are One - One in the Service of The Father Solen Aum Solen - for We Two - are one and the same WILL made manifest -- We have no will save His - - His Will is Ours - - in Him We have Our Being - and Our Life is His - - therefore We serve with all of our being - for We Know Him as the Cause of Our BEing -- So be it that in Him We are One --

Let this be Mine Word unto thee - - so be it I shall return at another hour --

Sori Sori -- The time is now - the hour is come for that which is to be done - and it is that which is to be done that matters - the Work at hand is the Great concern -- So be it that We of the Host are not unmindful of thee - or of thine time - and thy comfort -- We see thee discomforted - and We see thee as one which hast given of thyself that ye might serve the Light - that "they" be blest -- So be it that We see thee as one prepared to do that which is given unto thee to do -- We see thee as one qualified - and too - We see thee as one now prepared for a Greater part - for thy passport hast been approved -- So be it and Selah The time is propitious that I say unto thee: The Way is now made clear for thy passage into the place wherein "they" dare not go - for "they" are as ones fearful - and they are unprepared to enter in -- "They" are as ones which have been troubled by fear of the unknown - that which they understand not --

It is said - that "they" fear not the darkness which binds "them" - yet they fear the Light which would be unto them their freedom - - this is of grave concern unto Us --

"They" have not been as ones prepared to have greater things revealed unto them - for they could not bear it - - they would be as the babe within the storm - unprepared to care for itself -- Therefore it is said: "Be ye prepared"- - none other enters into the border of the Realm of Mine abode - for I say: It is the far distant land from thine - of other realms - other time bands - wherein We count not the hours - the days, the years - - all time is counted by events of the Cosmos --

Now it is come when there are ones which are prepared to be brot out of the place wherein ye are - and ye shall find that these are no strangers unto thee - for ye have sat in Council with them - and ye have been as One with them - - and ye have given of thyself that they be blest even as they have blest thee -- So be it and Selah --

While I say ye have sat in Council with them - ye have counseled together that all be blest -- Changes have been made in thy world - in the world of men - - by the Work which is done within these Council Chambers - which "they" know not of - for the world of men is the - and the Way of Spirit - which is the Greater part - is the - and it comes under the direction of this Council with which ye are an Associate -- There are many which are associated with this Council 5 - - while the Council of Councils is the OVER ALL COUNCIL to which it looks - and is responsible - - such I would have thee Know -- So be it that I say unto thee: Be ye as one prepared to enter into the Greater part - for there are many places wherein ye shall serve - - and be it known that thy part is no small part - thy work but begun -- So be it We shall continue this at a later hour --

Sori Sori -- This is the time in which We shall come together for this Word - - and it shall be as the Word held for this time -- There be the ones which come into flesh as infants born of woman - - these are the ones which have volunteered for a part -- Yet as they enter into the realm of flesh - they are prone to forgetfulness - - these are as the ones which lose their way -- While there are ones which come by <u>other means</u> - - these come as travelers - fully aware of their Mission - their part - and they Know from whence they came - and whither they goest. So be it that these are as the Initiate - which walks softly in the House of the Lord -- They boast not - neither do they flount themself before the unlearned - - they are mindful of their part - they fear nought - they feign not great and wise sayings - - they are the wise ones - they are the ones which Know their part well - they Know them which are prepared to receive - and "them" which have not the mind to receive -- They are the Guardians of Truth and Justice - and they are not want for the proper Word - yet they speak only when wise and prudent -- So be it that ye shall come to Know that which hast been said - and ye shall be as one prepared to do a Greater Work - for there is much to be done -- So be it and Selah --

* * *

Sori Sori -- The way is now prepared before thee - and ye shall enter in and ye shall be glad for thy part - for thou hast been faithful in all things and ye have been obedient unto the Call - - and not any time hast thou betrayed thyself -- So be it - ye shall be glad for thy preparation --

= **The Blessing** =

Sori Sori -- Mine hand I place upon thy head in Holy Benediction - - I pronounce the Word which shall bless thee -- So be it and Selah --

Give unto thyself the rest needed - and I shall speak unto thee at another hour -- So be it and Selah --

= **The Chosen Path** =

Sori Sori -- This is Mine time - and I shall speak of the ways of the Initiate - which are the ones which overcome - the ones which have won their Victory --

The Victors are the Ones which have overcome the flesh - which hast <u>become</u> the victors thru great effort and patience - - they have brot forth the fruit of their labor - by their patience - - they have wearied not of their lot - they have not flinched from their lot - neither have they turned aside from their path (their chosen path) -- They have been true unto themself - their trust -- So be it and Selah -- Be ye as one prepared for another part - yet greater - - and the Greater the part - the Greater the responsibility - the Greater the Revelation -- So be it and Selah --

This is Mine Word unto thee at this hour --

* * *

Sori Sori -- This I would say unto thee at this time: Be ye as one prepared for thy new part - and it shall be given unto thee in parts -- So be it ye shall rest - and I shall speak unto thee later --

= Response =

Sori Sori -- Blest are they which are touched - and respond unto the touch -- It is the part given unto Me to touch thee - - thine to respond unto it -- So be it that I have touched thee at this hour - and ye have given of thineself that I might be unto thee Sibor - that I might bring unto thee Greater Knowledge of things which thou hast not known - that which is yet to come -- So be it that I am with thee that ye be <u>prepared</u> for the things yet to come --

I am now prepared to bless thee with such knowledge as ye have not had - or remembered - - ye <u>shall</u> remember -- So be it and Selah --

There is but One Lord God - and I Am He - and it is Mine part to bring thee out of bondage - and ye shall do thy part - and ye shall be as one free forever -- So be it and Selah -- The part which is given unto thee is <u>obedience</u> unto the law - - Mine part is to give unto thee the law and show thee the way unto the Father's House -- That which is given unto thee is given freely and without stint - - it is proffered unto all men yet they accept it not - while thou hast accepted it in great measure --

I say: The fullness thou hast not comprehended - for thy <u>learning</u> - thy <u>Work</u> is not yet finished -- Thy part is increased according to thy capacity - thy time - and it behooves Me to Know thy time and thy capacity - that ye be not given more than ye can bear --

So be it that ye shall be as one prepared to receive in Greater measure - - So let it be - and it shall be as ye are prepared --

= Expansion of Capacity =

Sori Sori -- Blest art thou - blest shall ye be - for I come that ye be blest. So be it and Selah -- The Part which is given unto thee shall expand and expand - for this have I said: "Be ye as one prepared for the Greater Part"--

Now ye shall begin a new book - and it shall be as a <u>New</u> one - for it shall be as a Greater Light - Greater Power - Greater Revelation - and it shall bring forth Greater Knowledge - for the ones which have the mind to follow Me -- So be it and Selah --

= Protection =

Forget not that there are many which would speak - for the time is now come when many are prepared to come as "The Voice in the Wilderness" - and it is now propitious that I say unto thee: They are the ones which are <u>prepared</u> - for it is said: "None pass without the proper credentials - none enter into thy place of abode without the Seal which I place upon them" - for they which bear not Mine Seal - shall not enter within thine place of abode -- So be it that they which enter shall bear Mine Seal - for their passports shall be in order - be approved by the Mighty Council -- So be it and Selah --

Put forth thy hand and receive them which are prepared to speak unto thee - - they shall speak for the Good of All - so let them speak - - and let it be well with thee -- So be it and Selah --

Recorded by Sister Thedra

Mission Statement

Give the truth to the world. Let it be received where it will. Many will read the messages. Some will accept the truth, others will read through curiosity, a few will ridicule. Yet to all is the truth given, and to all remains the power of choice.

The hope of the world in these times is in spiritualizing all forms of activity---promoting understanding through love and service. These must be the watchwords if the world is to come into lasting peace. We are trying to influence a world that is going astray and could cause undreamed of suffering. We are trying to overcome the thought of materialists and to bring a spiritual outlook into the earthly life. We need the help of all on earth who can think in spiritual terms. The great battle to be fought now is between the spiritual and the material, between idealism and carnalism. You can help by spreading the word---we are asking that you help because the battle may be long and the victory far away.

Halls of Light is not allied with any sect, denomination, political entity, organization, neither endorses nor opposes any cause. There are no dues for membership. Halls of Light is self-supporting through its own voluntary contributions. Halls of Light has but one purpose: to help through encouragement and understanding...

To contact the publishers or to obtain copies of our other books, please contact us at email: goldtown11@gmail.com

Sananda's Appearance

Be ye as one which hast heard Mine Voice and responded unto it - for I speak that ye hear, and I say that which is wise and prudent.

Let it be known that I, the Lord thy God hast spoken and bear ye witness of Me, for I have made manifest Mineself that ye might know Me - and for this wast these manifestations made.

I say that I have made Mineself manifest that ye might see Me with thine mortal eyes; that ye might bear witness of Me. Yet thine companions saw and believed not; neither did they hear, for they were selfish and unprepared - yet, did I deny them?

I say; I came that they which would might see and hear. I went and came again unto Mine own. So be it that I have found; I have given unto the found that they which know not might know; that they might come to know as thou knowest.

Yet, how many hast turned from Me and persecuted thee for Mine Word. It is said, "Woe unto them which persecute Mine servants." is it not the law which they set into motion?

Yea Mine beloved, I say they bring about their own downfall. So be it that I am a compassionate one, and I would that they know what they do. So be it they shall learn well their lessons. So let it be, for this is the mercy of God, the One which hast sent Me.

So be it. I AM The Wayshower, the Lord thy God

I AM Sanand

About the Late Sister Thedra

Since the later part of the last Century, the Kumara wisdom has begun to reemerge into the world. This process began with the late Sister Thedra, whom Jesus Christ appeared physically to while on her deathbed and spontaneously healed her of cancer while she was in the Yucatan, where she had gone to accept her fate and the will of our Lord Jesus Christ.

That is when something miraculous occurred. Jesus spoke to her saying, "My name is Esu Sananda Kumara" and then sent Thedra down to the Monastery of the Seven Rays in Peru to learn the Kumara wisdom. After five years, Thedra was told to return to the United States where she founded the Association of Sananda and Sanat Kumara at Mt. Shasta in California.

While heading this organization, Thedra channeled many messages from Sananda and taught the Kumara wisdom. He introduced himself to her by his true name, "Sananda Kumara" And it was by his command that Sister Thedra went to Peru but eventually left upon being told that her experience there was complete. She then traveled to Mt. Shasta in California and founded the Association of Sananda and Sanat Kumara. A.S.S.K.

You ask, Is There a difference between Jesus and Sananda? Our Lord's name given at birth by his Father Joseph and his beloved mother Mary was Yeshua, thus being of the house of David and the order of Yoseph, he would be called Yeshua ben Yoseph. The Roman Emperors placed the name of Jesus upon the sir name of Yeshua after the Emperor Justinian adopted Christianity as the official faith of Rome and ordered that the sacred books be compiled upon approval of a specially appointed counsel appointed by the Emperor into a recognizable and uniform work titled "The Bible". Prior to this, there never was a Bible per se.

There existed until the time of the Emperor's edict, a selection of many Sacred texts that were employed in the Sacred Teachings, many of which were copies of what the Greeks had transposed from the original texts in the Libraries of Alexandria which were originally compiled by Alexander the Great, and were destroyed by Julius Caesar, fearing that they might prove dangerous to the rule of a Caesar, an Earthly God.

In addition, it was to keep the knowledge of Alexander's Libraries out of the hands of the Ptolemy's who were said to be descended from his bloodline. At the time, Caesar had no way of knowing that vast portions of the Library were already in the Americas, in the Great Universities of the Inca, and in possession of the Mayans.

Yeshua spent many years in the East after his ascension. The Good Sheppard, upon his appearances to the Apostles after his ascension, told them that he was going to tend to his Father's other sheep; which meant, plainly, that he was continuing upon his sacred journey. As The Ascended One, Yeshua took to himself the name of Sananda, meaning the Christed One, and Sananda was thus embraced forevermore by the Great Solar Brotherhood. To many of you this is all new, to others it will be received as a welcome easing of the wall that has so long separated two sides of the same coin. This is being placed into the ethers and the matrix of thought at this time, as it is the time of The Great Awakening, and the Christos is already emerging into the new consciousness.

Authority to use the name of Sananda was given to Sister Thedra when Jesus, (Sananda), appeared to her in the Yucatan and cured her instantly of the cancer that had taken over her body. Further, he allowed a picture of his countenance to be taken at that time that she might realize the occurrence was more than a dream. Thedra had a large format camera called a 620 that she used to take the picture of Sananda.

Sanada's Message to her by Sister Thedra: "Sori Sori: Mine hand I have placed upon thine head, and I have given unto thee the authority to use Mine name. Give unto them the name Sananda, by which they shall know Me as the Lord thy God - the Son of God, sent that ye be made to know me, the One sent from out The Inner Temple that there be Light in the world of men. Now it is come when ones which have the will to follow Me shall come to know Me by that name which I commanded thee to give unto the world as Mine New name.

There are many that shall call upon the name of Jesus, yet they will deny the new name as they are want to do. Unto thee I give assurance that I am the One sent that there be Light in the world of men. Now let this be understood, that they that deny Mine New Name deny Me by any name. So be it I have appointed thee Mine spokesman; I've given unto thee the power and authority to speak for being that which I AM. And I say unto thee Mine child whom I have called forth and anointed thee with the Holy Spirit, thy name shall be as it is now called, Thedra, that name I spoke unto thee from out the ethers, and thou heard Me and accepted that which I gave unto thee; and wherein have I deceived thee? Wherein have I forgotten thee, or left thee alone?"

I say unto thee: "Mine hand is upon thee and I shall sustain thee and you shall come to know that which I have kept for thee. So be it that I have kept thy reward, and at no time shall it be dissipated or scattered, for it is intact. So let this Mine Word suffice them which question thee - let them question, and I shall bear witness for thee. For do I not know Mine servants from the traitors? Do I not reward Mine servants according unto their works or merits? I speak that they might know that I am mindful of Mine servants, that I am not a poor puny priest who has forgotten his servants.

"I say unto them: Mine servants shall be glorified above the crowned heads of the nations which have set themselves apart, and denied Me Mine part of Mine word for they have turned from Me in their conceit and forgetfulness. Now let this go on record as Mine Word, and I shall give unto them proof, which are of a mind to follow Me.

So be it as I have spoken and I am not finished; I shall speak again and again, and I shall rise Mine Voice against them which set foot against Mine servants, and they shall be as ones cast out. So let them ask of Me and I shall enlighten them. So be it I know whereof I speak. Be ye as ones blest to accept Me and know Me for that which I AM." On Saturday, June 13, 1992, at exactly 10.00 PM, at the age of 92, Sister Thedra made her final transition from the comfort of her own bed. When the time arrived, she simply took one small breath and slipped quietly away, without pomp or fanfare.

She left as she had lived: as a humble servant for the greater good. The messages included were given to Sister Thedra shortly before her transition. They are compiled here to give you some idea of the significance of her passing and of the expansion of the work, as she is now free of the physical limitations and the pain of the past. Her work now in the higher realms will simply be an extension of that work.

Divine Explanations

Part - I

The following explanations and definitions of terms used by Sananda (Jesus) and the various Sibors were given by Sananda through direct revelation. They are not alphabetical. These explanations should be read over and over.

- - - - - - - - - - -

"My Beloved Sibors please give us plainly the definitions of the following words that there may be no error on our part." - Thedra.

THEMSELF? What is the explanation of your terminology of "Themself" – "themselves"?

"I (Sananda) say unto thee mine beloved, they which would be unto thee a vessel, unto thee a sibor, unto thee teacher, are as ones enlightened of the Father, enlightened of the Father for the light is in them.

They know their parts well, they have their memory, they have mastered the elements, they can do all the things which I do and they take unto "themself" no credit for they have overcome self. They are self-less. Now I say unto them: them which work with thee are the Selfless ones. They ask <u>no</u>thing for "themself." Now while this is true they are as one.

They are within the great brotherhood of the Selfless Ones - the Ones clothed in white. They are as the Royal Assembly - and each unto his own, yet each for all and all for one. Now while in thy world, they (of thy world) are <u>selfish</u> and they are not for the whole - they ask for self and I speak of these as the selfish ones. I speak unto them in terms which they shall come to know and therein is wisdom.

I say that they shall be responsible for "themself" and as a world of me I say they shall be responsible for their society; they "themself" have created it. Now I speak unto thee mine beloved, I say "ye shall be responsible for thyself. He shall be responsible for himself. They as a whole shall be responsible for that which they have created, while thou art responsible unto thyself for thine part - and not held accountable for theirs. Be it so."

BELEIS? "Mighty is the word and great the power thereof. I say unto thee this word carries with it the part of surrender. The word is the release of power - that which is sent forth by the one which asks of the Father His blessing. It is the surrender of the self - the complete surrender of the personal will and letting the Father's will be accomplished in all things through thee. "<u>So</u> <u>be</u> <u>it</u>" - it the accomplishment, the acceptance of the Father's plan."

SELAH? - "The word carries the Seal of Truth - meaning it is without error - no mistake - it is the verification of Truth - not subject to change.

SIBET? – "The Sibet is one which has offered or presented himself as a candidate for the greater learning and for the greater initiation. He comes as an empty vessel that he may be filled. So be it."

SIBOR? - "I am the Sibor of Sibors." - "The Sibor is one which has been illumined of God the Father. He has returned unto the Father purified. He has gone the Royal Road - which means he has overcome death. He has mastered the lower elements - he controls the elements. He can raise the dead - heal the sick - he can create like unto the Father for he has finished his course and won the victory and returned unto the Father the Victor. So be it."

"I am the Sibor of Sibors. I am the first born of Him which hast sent me. Sananda."

LEGIRONS? - "Beloved - I say unto thee: thy opinions and thy dogmas are not the least of these - neither thy creeds. Be it ever that these are great and heavy ones. Now let it be understood that a leg-iron is something which holds thee bound. It is something which holds thee, it keeps thee fast, wherein progress is not possible. Now that progress be made possible, ye shall cut away the legirons.

Knowest thou these bound by legirons? These are to be pitied, they drag them with them, impeding their progress - and they are as ones bound! They are not free - are they? While they serve their sentence - they are as ones bound - they are bond-men - they are bound men - men bound. Now let me say I too am a "bondsman." I came that they may be free. I say I bring unto thee the law which thou shall obey - unto the letter - then I shall give unto thee that which I have kept for thee. Be ye as one prepared for that.

PREPARATION? Now - preparation - what do you mean by "preparation?" "This my beloved is the part which they shall do - the part of preparation is: cleaning thyself of all the opinions, indoctrinations of man. The cup must be emptied. This is thy part, the becoming the '"little child" unopinionated, unscathed and unmarred with or by their doctrines, creeds and crafts. I say the child is unindoctrinated and un-opionated and is the virgin mind – (yet it does not remain so long in this world). While the little child represents the empty cup - the empty vessel, the Virgin Spirit, it is given unto the child to be one which has come from other realms and to have been in many embodiments, many times: yet the symbol of virginity. Wherein is it said there are none innocent among thee?

WHEREIN I AM? - "Now while thou art yet within the world of men - I am within mine Father's realm, the place wherein there is no darkness, wherein <u>ALL</u> things are known. I say wherein <u>ALL</u> things are known, wherein there is <u>No</u> mystery.

And too - I say when thou hast attained unto thy Royal Road, when thou hast become part of the Royal Assembly, thou shall know as I - thou shall be as I - thou shall be brought into the place wherein I am, for I say unto thee this is attainment. This is the day of Attainment, the day of "becoming," the day of thy salvation. Know ye that this is Mine day - the day for which thou hast waited? I say unto thee: "This is the day of fulfillment. This is Mine Day. Mine Day is come ---"

What is meant by "ALL THE LANDS OF THE EARTH?"- "This I mean, all the lands of the Earth. I have said it, I mean it as I have said it and there is no mystery of or to it."

ALL MANKIND? "This is Mine people - Mine children - Mine flock - Mine Church - Mine brethren - Mine congregation unto whom I shall minister. By Mine own hand shall they be fed and led. These have I came to find. Are not all <u>hu</u>-man beings considered "Man kind"? by thine own standards. Yet all men are not of me."

WHAT DO YOU MEAN - "WILL IT SO"? - "There is power in the "WILL" and the power which they use to create their own torment and confusion is misused energy. Yet they will this - they will it so. Now when ye will to serve me ye give unto me thy undivided attention, the whole heart - thy heart - thine ALL. Yet I say that they which doth attempt to serve me with one hand and the dragon with the other has not willed to serve me. They are not of me - they are not of Mine flock. I say they are either with me or against me. I cannot accept the one hand while they reserve the other for the dragon. They are not wholeheartedly mine.

I make no compromises with the dragon. Mine shall come out from them and surrender unto me themself - their all - without reservation. This is willing it so - for they will the Father's will be done in them, through them, by them. They leave no energy that the dragon may use. They use all their energy to serve me. This is mine word unto thee."

WHAT IS DARKNESS? - "Thine Un-Knowing - thy darkness comes from the fall of man - which one was with God the Father perfect which didst have his memory blanked from him when he didst transgress."

MAYAS VEIL? - "The result of such unknowing - the darkness which man has brought upon himself. The part he has created for himself."

WHAT DOES IT MEAN TO <u>BETRAY ONES SELF</u>? - "This is the sad part for first the 'fall' came from his betrayal - and it hast resulted in the fall - in the veil of Maya - the "illusion" and in thy un-knowing - in thy own darkness."

WHAT OF BETRAYING "HIS OWN TRUST"? - "The plan is all inclusive and includes <u>all</u> - yet there are ones unaware of the "plan" - (and they are not as included in this temple as yet) - no personal reference unto the ones within this temple. Now when one becomes aware of his part, he is given the law and it is provided for his own good and he has the law clearly stated, plainly recorded, and he turns his face away - that he may hide from it. He puts his fingers into his ears that he may not hear it. He gives unto his benefactors the bitter cup and he goes his own willful way.

He has betrayed himself for he shall be caught up short of his course. When he has been given a chance - a "part" within the plan and he has committed himself, he has the responsibility given unto him for that "part" and should he be so foolish as to betray his trust he shall be like unto one which has thrown overboard his <u>own</u> life belt - poor foolish ones!"

WISDOM? - What is meant by the word "Wisdom?" - "Wisdom is that which is light, the knowledge of the law and its proper use. The right use of the law - and this Mine children is Mine part. I come that ye may BECOME wise! Wisdom is thy divine gift - not of man, for man of Earth is foolish indeed - and he is nothing save that which the Father has endowed him. All else is of the world of "illusion" which shall pass into nothingness in the Light which I Am."

WHAT IS THE "PEARL OF GREAT PRICE, THE PRICELESS PEARL? - "That which I offer thee - thy freedom, thy salvation from bondage - thine inheritance in full - Mine word which is not purchased with coin - not bought, neither is it sold. It is the wisdom of which I speak. Mine offer unto thee is without price - it is the 'pearl' - "Mine Pearl."

WHY ARE MIS-SPELLED AND GRAMMATICAL ERRORS USED IN THESE SCRIPTS? - "I am not a conformist. I am not concerned with the letters of man for I am He which has come that they be unbound by their fetters. I say unto them which desireth the letter - unto them the letter.

I say unto thee: be ye as ones free from such bondage. I stand ready to free thee from thy bondage. Unto thee I say - give unto the letter no thought. <u>Hear</u> what I <u>say</u> for I shall say it in many ways as becomes me and serves mine purpose. I say I am no stranger in thine midst. While they know me not, I know them. I see them bowing down before the Golden Calf - and they worship at the shrines which they have set up. (Their own standards of education.) They guild them and bring unto them burnt offerings - yet they close me out.

Be ye not so foolish. <u>Be</u> <u>ye</u> <u>not</u> <u>so</u> <u>foolish</u>! I am come that ye might have Light - Wisdom - Freedom which is the Father's will. While the letter changeth and passeth away - and the letter is not the law - the letter is of no consequence other than to cause thee to see the "Word." The word is the power which shall provoke thine mind into action and thy mind shall be free from the letter. See what is meant within the Word, and let thine mind be staid on <u>me</u> - the Light, the Way - Truth and Wisdom."

"I am He which hast come - that ye be free: forever free. I am Sananda - Son of God. Once known as the Nazarine, He which was born of Mary, Ward of Joseph.

Recorded by Thedra

Part - 2

THE WHITE BROTHERHOOD AND THE EMERALD CROSS.

THE MANY QUESTIONS ABOUT THE WHITE BROTHERHOOD AND THE ORDER OF THE EMERALD CROSS MAY BE EXPLAINED IN A FEW SIMPLE WORDS.

ONE HAS TO EARN THE RIGHT TO BECOME A MEMBER - EITHER IN THIS LIFE OR OTHERS BEFORE OR AFTER - NONE ENTER UNPREPARED.

THE WHITE BROTHERHOOD - or - THE ROYAL ASSEMBLY is of the Realms of Light---not of Earth. The Ascended Masters have proven themself in the school of Earth (THE SCHOOL FOR GODS) who have trodden the path of INITIATION - overcome the trials and temptations of the mundane world - who have gained their freedom and ascended as the Lord Jesus Christ (Sananda). They have gone the ROYAL ROAD.

Knowing the path of the Initiate -- and its pitfalls -- and sorrow, they extend a hand in Fellowship - LOVE and WISDOM - NEVER depriving the candidate an opportunity to learn his lessons well -- for this is His salvation -- for this do they proffer their hand, NOT to do our part for us, but rather that we become strong and free by our own strength.

The Royal Assembly or the White Brotherhood have known all of the heartaches, the longing, crucifications, temptations and JOYS of the aspirant -- the candidate -- the Master -- the Sibor -- herein lies their strength, their understanding, their great love for us on the path.

Their love and understanding knows no bounds. They give help when necessary for our progress. They also withhold it wisely - should it deprive us of our lessons. The candidate on the path of initiation shall become self-responsible for all his actions -- all the energy allotted him throughout his whole EARTHLY existence - and make atonement for all his misused energy, for therein is his salvation.

There is no one else which will ever make this atonement for us (the candidate) on the path of unfoldment. While the host of "WHITE BROTHERS" Brothers of LIGHT are ready to assist, the candidate shall (MUST) put forth every effort to overcome all the forces of darkness which would deter his progress and earn for himself his freedom from BONDAGE.

THE EMERALD CROSS

THE EMERALD CROSS is a company – and an order of beings who work within the Brotherhood of MAN - and the Fatherhood of God - for the good of all mankind --- And at the head of this group is one known as MOTHER SARAH, the personification of love -- embodiment of all MOTHERS. That is: the LOVE of God made Manifest - in MOTHERS. The blessed Mother Sarah is the head of this Order of the Emerald Cross. And when one earns the Divine right and privileges to associate themselves with this Order, it is the joy of all the Orders - and Brothers of Light. I speak for the Order - for I am known as Merseda. (As told to Sister Thedra of the Order of the Emerald Cross).

COMANCHE - which is the porter at the door - which doth keep out the unworthy, the unjust, the unclean. The Door Keeper - the one responsible for the Temple Gate.

BITTER CUP - that which you would not like to partake of - that which poisons thee, that which is not good, that which torments thee - that which ye have given unto thy brother to torment him which returns unto thee as a boomerang to torment thee - which ye shall receive multiplied - which has accumulated in its swift flight. I say prepare not for thyself the bitter cup for ye shall drink of the portion which thou doth prepare for thy brother. Be ye not foolish - make it not bitter.

BLEST OF MINE BEING - I have given of Mine self that Mine beloved has being.

BLEST OF MINE PRESENCE - Have I not gone the long way? I have gone out from Mine place of abode that I might bring light unto the Earth that she might be lifted up - that the children thereof might be delivered of all bondage - that they might return unto the place from whence they went out. And have I not come unto thee many times that this be accomplished? Have I not done all which has been given unto me to do? Wherein have I failed thee? Have I not done all that I have come to do? - While it is not as yet finished, I shall not fail. My mission shall be finished ere I return unto Mine abiding place. Shall I not be unto the true and shall I not return the Victor?

GAVE OF HIMSELF - Did I not give of Mine Self - hast thou? Have I not been true unto Mine trust? Have I asked aught for Myself? Have I not done that which I have promised? Have I not given Mine All? Have I not come on a Sacrificial Mission? What more have I to give - other than myself?

PORE - The physical body - vehicle which thou dost use.

<u>INITIATION</u> - Thy preparation for the inner temple. Each step is an initiation. One step at a time - the overcoming of self - the world - the becoming that which I am.

<u>COSMOS</u> - That which is unseen throughout many universes by thy eyes. Great is the expanse of the Father's Kingdom and the total thereof is referred to as "throughout the Cosmos."

<u>LORD'S</u> <u>STRANGE</u> <u>ACT</u> - This I shall reveal in Mine own time.

<u>WALK</u> <u>WHICH</u> <u>WAY</u> <u>THY</u> <u>CROWN</u> <u>TILTS</u> <u>NOT</u> - as a Son of God. Do honor unto thy Father Mother God - and thou shall be as one which has the Royal Raiment upon thine shoulders - and ye shall wear it in honor and with dignity.

<u>WHEN</u> <u>IT</u> <u>SAYS</u> <u>IT</u> <u>IS</u> <u>RECORDED</u> - <u>WHEREIN</u> <u>IS</u> <u>IT</u> <u>RECORDED</u>? - In the secret place - in the eth - and within the inner temple - and wherein thou art are many things recorded - which I do speak of. Ye shall see these recordings when thou doth enter into the secret place of Mine abode. I say ye shall read the records wherein are written the records of all thy travels from the time ye left the Father Mother God until thine return unto him.

<u>WHAT</u> <u>IS</u> <u>MICHAEL'S</u> <u>FLAMING</u> <u>SWORD</u>? - "The "Sword of Truth and justice."

Recorded by Sister Thedra

Other Books by TNT Publishing

Who am I and Why Am I here?

The Significance of Existence

Death and the Incredible Life After

Fear of Death Removed

Paradise Regained

Spiritual Laws Revealed

Unseen Forces

Too Good to Be True

The Truth of Life in the Spirit World

He Who Has Ears

The Great Awakening, Volumes I thru VII

The Great Awakening, Volume VIII,
THE WHITE STAR OF THE EAST

The Great Awakening, Volume IX,
I THE LORD GOD SAY UNTO THEM

The Great Awakening, Volume X,
MINE INTERCOM MESSAGES FROM THE REALMS OF LIGHT

The Great Awakening, Volume XI,
THE BOOK OF THE LORD

The Great Awakening, Volume XII thru XV,
TEMPLE TEACHINGS FROM THE HIGHER REALMS

Transfiguration Volumes I thru Volume VIII

Contact us at

Email: goldtown11@gmail.com

Web: https://www.whoamiandwhyamihere.com/order-online

www.ingramcontent.com/pod-product-compliance
Lightning Source LLC
LaVergne TN
LVHW051556070426
835507LV00021B/2614